52
SIMPLE WAYS
TO · TEACH
YOUR CHILD
ABOUT
GOD

52
SIMPLE WAYS
TO·TEACH
YOUR CHILD
ABOUT
GOD

Todd Temple

A Division of Thomas Nelson Publishers
NASHVILLE

To
Doug Fields
Master Picture Taker

Published in Nashville, Tennessee, by Oliver-Nelson Books, a division of Thomas Nelson, Inc., Publishers, and distributed in Canada by Lawson Falle, Ltd., Cambridge, Ontario.

Scripture quotations are taken from the HOLY BIBLE: NEW INTERNATIONAL VERSION. Copyright © 1973, 1978, 1984 by the International Bible Society. Used by permission of Zondervan Bible Publishers.

Printed in the United States of America.
ISBN 0-8407-9589-0

1   2   3   4   5   6—96   95   94   93   92   91

◆ Contents

◆ How to Use These Ideas

This isn't a book of Sunday school lessons about God. It doesn't contain memory verses, Bible quizzes, or homework. There are no lesson plans, summary statements, or materials-needed lists.

Forget all the classroom stuff—these are simple activities that help you open up discussions about God with your child. Each idea helps you create a picture of one aspect of God's character. Here's how to get started:

Step One   *Pick.* Select any idea that interests you. You don't need to go through the book in order (the ideas are arranged alphabetically)— each one is its own picture of God.

Step Two   *Read.* Each idea starts by showing *you* —the parent—how God is like the image described by the title (e.g., "God Is Like an Artist"). Then it suggests an activity to help you convey that picture to your child.

Step Three *Change.* Fiddle with the activity so that it fits your child's maturity, skills, and interests. If you don't, some of the ideas may shoot over her head; others will seem childish.* You know your child best—design the activity with her in mind. The discussion questions are just suggestions; feel the freedom to use or discard them as you choose. Also, although most of the ideas are written as one-on-one activities, they can work with two children or as activities for the whole family.

Many of the ideas include an "Other Perspectives" section; here additional activities are described that relate to the picture. You may wish to follow up the main activity with one of these later on. Also, if the

---

* *A note about language:* You may be a father or a mother using these ideas with your son or daughter. So rather than create tiresome sentences like "The parent should keep his or her opinion to him/herself at first so that the child can feel free to express his or her own," I stick with one sex or the other. Some ideas are written with the child as a son, others as a daughter. Either way, the ideas will work with boys or girls.

main idea is impractical for you, maybe an activity in this section will work in its place.

Each idea begins with a Bible verse that suggests the image of God conveyed in the activity. You may wish to use this verse in the discussion. A "Self-Portraits" section concludes many of the ideas. It contains other verses that may help you convey the picture.

1 ◆ God Is Like An Artist

Go on an Art Excursion

The heavens declare the glory of God;
the skies proclaim the work of
his hands.   (Psalm 19:1)

Why did God make things so beautiful? He didn't have to. He could have done much worse. He could have made all flowers smell like mildew, all trees gray, all foods taste like cabbage. He might have made all animals identical, every sunset look the same, all seasons equal, the temperature a steady forty degrees year-round.

But God isn't a factory; He's an artist.

When He painted the world, He used a palette containing every color, pattern, shape, texture, odor, taste, and sound. Why so much variety? Maybe He figured He'd have to stare at it for a few years, so He might as well make it interesting. Maybe He figured He was the master artist and we were to be His students, and so He wanted to inspire us.

Or, maybe God uses His art as windows through which we can catch a glimpse of the artist. We can find pictures of His character in His creation.

Art Critics   Visit the library and pick up two books, one containing photos of sculptures or paintings and the other containing photographs of nature.

Look through the first book with your child, stopping periodically to discuss a work of art: "What do you think of this painting [or sculpture]?" "What do you think the artist was trying to tell us?" "What do you think the artist was like? Happy? Sad? Angry? Overwhelmed?" "Why do you think so?" With older children, you can read about one artist and try to see how his art relates to his life. The point is to help your child use the art as a window into the character of its artist. Do this with a few pieces.

Now look at the nature photos. Explain that God, too, is an artist. While looking together at various photos of animals, plants, and landscapes, ask your child the same kinds of questions as before. It's important to encourage her to describe the Artist as revealed in his art—not simply the God she's learned about in Sunday school.

Here are some words you and your child may come up with: *complex, genius, sensitive, delicate, quiet, dangerous, fearless, strong, big, funny.*

Other Perspectives   *Art Hike.*   Instead of looking for God's work in books, observe it in a natural setting or at a zoo.

2 ◆ God Is Like a Baby

Conduct a Baby Exam

Today in the town of David a Savior has been born to you; he is Christ the Lord. This will be a sign to you: You will find a baby wrapped in cloths and lying in a manger. (Luke 2:11–12)

God in Diapers Let's face it: Jesus *could* have made a more impressive entrance onto planet Earth. He could have whizzed in on a meteorite. Or skied down a lightning bolt. He could have ridden through the streets on a Bengal tiger or soared in on a giant eagle. (If He had, playing Jesus in the annual Christmas play would certainly be more fun.)

Jesus *could* have arrived in style. Instead, He showed up in a barn.

He was naked and bloody, a crying, drooling, red-faced, puffy-cheeked, helpless newborn baby. They cut His umbilical cord, wrapped Him in cloth, and stuck Him in an animal feed trough. So there you have it: God, Creator of Universe, King of Entire World, makes His grand entrance onto Earth as a thumb-sucking, dirty-diapered infant, born in a barn. (Hence, his habit of forgetting to shut doors.) Jesus didn't just drop out of the sky *disguised* as a human.

He *was* a human, and He arrived here just like everyone else. He even had a belly button to prove it.

Baby Doc   To help your child understand the significance of this God-as-baby concept, conduct a baby exam. A baby brother or sister will do, or you can borrow a friend's infant. You'll need the baby's parent's help with some of the questions. You'll also need some equipment: cloth tape measure (such as a tailor uses), scale, baby toy, a pen. Be sure to wash your hands before beginning the exam. Working together, complete the information form at the end of this section.

When you've completed the exam, serve milk and cookies (or a jar of applesauce) in the baby's nursery and discuss babyhood. Don't look for "right" answers here; just try to get your child to picture Jesus as a real live baby.

Ask: Why do babies cry? Why do they like to be held so much? Why is their skin so soft? With all the crying, dirty diapers, doctor bills, sleepless nights, and snotty noses, why do grown-ups want to have babies? Why does God have us arrive as babies instead of as grown-ups?

Now read together the story of the first Christmas from Luke 2:1–12. Talk about the story: Why did they wrap Jesus in cloths? Why did they put Him in a feed trough (manger)? Did Jesus have a belly button? What kind? Do you think Jesus ever dirtied His diapers? Why did God decide to show up on earth as a baby instead of as a grown-up?

Explain how helpless infants are: When they're cold, they can't put on more clothes or pull up their blanket. When they're hungry, they can't go to the fridge and make a peanut butter sandwich. When they're thirsty, they can't run down to 7-Eleven for a Slurpie. They can't crawl over to get a toy they want, and they can't run out of the house if there's a fire. They can't really do anything for themselves. Without constant attention from other people, they'd die.

You might say something like this to your child: "Have you ever felt helpless? It's a scary feeling, isn't it? One of the reasons God became a helpless baby is that He wanted us to know that *He* knows what helplessness feels like. He knows what diaper rash feels like. He knows what it's like to be cold and not be able to pull up the blanket. He knows how scary it is to be alone in a dark room and hear strange sounds. He knows what it's like to be helpless. So the next time you're feeling helpless or frightened or lonely, talk to Jesus. You can say, 'Jesus, I'm feeling helpless. You know what that feels like, so can You please help me?' He knows exactly how you feel because He was little once too."

Other Perspectives

Gerber Time. Your child can get a better understanding of a baby's helplessness through role-playing. Let your child pretend to be a baby. Feed her a meal. During the meal she is not allowed to talk or point to show you what she wants to eat, nor can she feed herself. Serve her soft and mushy foods only and have her wear a bib (she still possesses one method of expressing distaste). After the meal talk about what she liked and didn't like. Ask her if it was frustrating not to be able to talk. Ask her what a baby does when she's had enough, or is still hungry, or doesn't like the strained carrots?

Baby Flashback.   Together, flip through your child's baby book. Tell her about the trip to the hospital, who came to visit, the list of names you considered, coming home for the first time, how the nursery looked, the child's first crawl, first word, first big laugh.

Baby Exam

Baby's Name _____

Birthdate: _____   Age _____ Months

Number of diaper changes per day: _____

Number of hours of sleep per day: _____

Number of times the baby usually
    wakes up in the night: _____

Weight: _____ pounds _____ ounces

Height: _____ inches

Length of index finger: _____ inches

Length of foot: _____ inches

Circumference of waist: _____ inches

Pulse: _____ beats per minute
    (count for six seconds, multiply by 10)

Grip-the-finger test:

    ☐ strong ☐ medium ☐ light

Eye tracking: Does the baby follow an object moving across its line of sight ☐ yes ☐ no ☐ kind of

The hair smells like *(check one)*
- ☐ shampoo
- ☐ soap
- ☐ hair gel
- ☐ a hamster cage
- ☐ no smell
- ☐ other:_____

Touch your tongue to the baby's arm: how does it taste?

(check one)
- ☐ salty
- ☐ oily
- ☐ soapy
- ☐ like anchovy pizza
- ☐ no taste
- ☐ other:_____

Examine the knee: how would you describe it
(check one)
- ☐ pudgy
- ☐ wrinkly
- ☐ cute
- ☐ wrinkly and pudgy but in a cute sort of way
- ☐ other_____

Check the belly button:
- ☐ inny
- ☐ outy
- ☐ can't tell yet
- ☐ no belly button (possibly an alien)

3 ◆ God Is Like a Best Friend

Build a Buddy

I no longer call you servants, because a servant does not know his master's business. Instead, I have called you friends, for everything that I learned from my Father I have made known to you. (Jesus, John 15:15)

Your best friend is one of those few people on the planet who knows all about you, and yet likes you anyway. That's pretty special, considering all the people who've only seen your *good* side and still aren't impressed.

One of the ingredients of best-friendship is letting another person look deep inside you—to see your dreams and fears, to learn your faults and strengths. When Jesus showed up, we humans got to see a side to God He'd never shown to anyone. We met a living, breathing Creator who laughed, cried, played, got mad, went for walks, hung out at parties, and told people what He was thinking. Suddenly, we could all have a new best friend.

Buddy Building Really good friends are hard to find. So why not help your child *build* a best friend? Use pillows and bunched-up towels to form the body, then dress the dummy in clothes. Draw the face on an old pillow case. If you're doing this as a family activity, pair off and build a couple of dummies.

Have your child name his ideal friend and give him a personality. Ask him to describe the buddy's favorite foods, music, sports, hobbies, TV shows, and heroes. To get him talking about the qualities of a best friend, have him describe what makes this friend so special. Ask, "How well does he listen? What's he do when others are putting you down behind your back? What's he do when you tell him a secret? Is there anything about you that you're afraid to tell him? If he found out the absolute worst things about you, would he still be your best friend?"

Now talk about God. "Jesus says He's our friend. But how do we know? Does He match up to our idea of a best friend? Could God ever qualify as your best friend? Does He listen? How do you know? Would He stop being your friend if He knew the worst stuff about you? If God were your best friend, how would He treat you? How would He want to be treated by you?"

It's tough to remain best friends with someone you seldom talk to. Take a moment so each of you can write a short thank-you note to God. The note should start off with "Dear Best Friend God," and then thank Him for things He does that make Him such a good friend. If you want, each of you can read your note.

Other Perspectives *Start a "Dear Best Friend God" Diary.* Encourage your child to start a prayer diary made up of thank-you notes and what's-going-on letters written to his best friend, Jesus. He doesn't have to worry about neatness or spelling or even putting a stamp on an envelope—the notes get "faxed" directly to God as he writes them.

Be a Better Friend. Ask your child to think of two steps he can take this week to be a better friend to someone he knows.

Friendly Proverbs. The book of Proverbs contains great advice on how to be a friend. Here are some helpful proverbs: 17:17, 18:13, 18:24, 20:19, 22:11, 27:6, 27:9,10.

Self-Portraits

> *Greater love has no one than this, that one lay down his life for his friends.*
> (Jesus, John 15:13)

> *If one falls down, his friend can help him up. But pity the man who falls and has no one to help him up!* (Ecclesiastes 4:10)

4 ◆ God Is Like A Big Sister or Brother

Talk Big

Whoever does God's will is my brother and sister and mother.   (Jesus, Mark 3:35)

Older siblings aren't always loving. Sometimes they can be downright mean. Like when your older brother starts a club with his friends and you want to join, so he makes a rule No Fourth Graders Allowed. You beg him, please can't he make an exception, and he talks it over with his friends and tells you there *is* one way to be in the club, but you have to (a) pour milk in your hair, (b) smear baby powder on your face, and (c) crawl around the block backwards on your hands and knees. So you pour, smear, and crawl, and then shout, "Yipee—I'm in the cluh-ub!" To which your brother and his friends chorus, "I quit!" and run off to start a new club—with no fourth graders allowed.

But this is an extreme case. Older siblings usually aren't *that* bad.

While big brothers and sisters can occasionally exploit their seniority, they really earn their rank when

we're being bullied. My big brother never had to battle any bullies for me. But I knew he was there, three
grades ahead of me and a whole lot stronger and
wiser, ready to stand by my side if I got into trouble.
That assurance made growing up a lot easier.

Jesus is like that. He doesn't fight our battles for
us—life has its share of scraped knees and bloodied
noses. But there's real comfort knowing that He's
there, ready to step in if things turn nasty. Woe to
anyone He catches messing with *His* kid brother or
sister.

Talk Big   Talk with your child about what it
means to be a big brother or sister. If your child has
an older sibling, ask: "What's the nicest thing your
big brother has ever done for you? Why did he do it?
How did it make you feel? Has he ever stood up for
you in front of other people? Why?"

If your child *is* a big brother or sister, ask: "Can
you think of the nicest thing you've ever done for
your little brother? Why did you do it? How did that
make you feel? Have you ever stood up for him when
he was being picked on? What made you do it? What
would you do if you saw him being beat up?"

Now talk about his older brother Jesus. Repeat the
child's answers to the question, "What does it mean
to be a big brother?" Ask: "Does Jesus act like an
older brother in any of these ways? How do you
think Jesus feels when He sees you in trouble? Why

doesn't He step in and fight all our battles for us? How can Jesus help you through life's tough times?"

Other Perspectives *Practice Siblinghood.* Talk further about the job of being a sibling. Ask your child to come up with two steps he can take this week to be a better brother or sister.

Be Big. Try to think of a younger child in your neighborhood who doesn't have an older sister or brother. Ask your child to consider acting the part.

5 ◆ God Is Like a Boss

Be the Boss

Well done, good and faithful servant! You have been faithful with a few things; I will put you in charge of many things. Come and share your master's happiness! (Matthew 25:21)

Take a quick walk through your home, and you can probably come up with at least a page of odd jobs that need to be done. But your to-do list looks easy when compared to what needs to be done outside your home: feed the hungry, stop hatred, educate children, clean up the air, heal the sick, and roughly a billion other tasks.

One reason God put us on the planet is to work for Him—to complete our share of this big to-do list. Those who show up to work find out that God is a great boss: He trains us, gives us tasks suited to our gifts and abilities, provides encouragement when we need it, and rewards us when we complete the work.

Big Promotion Kids understand a lot about being a worker, but they don't get many opportunities to be the boss. The next time you have a big household project to do—cleaning the garage, washing the windows, preparing for overnight guests—switch jobs with your child. Make her the boss and you the worker. Sit down together and make a list of all the specific tasks, then let her tell you who is supposed to do what. Then get to work!

Be sure to ask lots of questions and ask for her help throughout the job. Treat her like a real boss, and respect her authority. If you've modeled good management in the past, she'll encourage you, give you coffee breaks, and lend a hand. If you've been more of a dictator than a good boss, that's what you'll get from her.

When the work is done, talk about how she felt being the boss and how you felt being the worker.

Explain that God is our boss, and we are His workers. What jobs does He have for us? How do you find out what He wants done? How does He help us do them? Does He pay us? How? What do you think is God's definition of a good worker?

Wrap things up by asking her to think of one job God wants her to accomplish this week. What is it? When will she work on it? Will He pay her for it? How?

Other Perspectives *Junior Management.* Your child may be in a leadership position on a sports team or when looking after younger brothers and sisters. Have her describe her responsibilities, and ask her to think of one or two steps she can take to become a better leader.

6 ◆ God Is Like Bread

Hold a Bake Session

I am the bread of life.   (Jesus, John 6:48)

I still remember my favorite after-school TV snack.
It wasn't Hostess Twinkies, or Vanilla Wafers, or
Goldfish crackers. It was Wonder Bread. I'd take a
slice, peel off the crust and roll the rest into a white
doughy ball. Then I'd pop the ball into my mouth and
try to suck on it, without chewing, until the next TV
commercial. If the show was really suspenseful (Gilli-
gan spotting a ship, for instance), I'd devour a half-
dozen slices before the closing credits. I could have
eaten an entire loaf that way, but I never got a
chance: my brothers and sisters enjoyed the same
snack, so we'd run out of bread before we ran out of
hunger.

I somehow got over my craving for Wonder Bread,
but other cravings have taken its place. Now I hunger for new cars, electronic gadgets, tropical vaca-
tions, the constant approval of others. And I still run
out of "bread" before I run out of hunger.

Deep inside we're all hungry. Yet nothing on earth
seems to satisfy the hunger—not for long anyway.
Just as God gave us physical hunger to remind us we

must eat to survive, He gives us a spiritual hunger to tell us we need Him to truly live.

Hold a Bake Session   Spend an afternoon baking in the kitchen. If you have enough equipment, make several loaves of bread and give some away to friends. While the bread is baking, sit down with your child and talk about hunger: How do we know when we are hungry? Why do our bodies work this way? What happens if we don't eat when we are hungry?

Talk about other things people crave. For instance, when someone is acting obnoxiously, we say he's "starved for attention." Can your child think of other things people crave (love, alcohol, drugs, gambling, money, new clothes, cars)? We get hungry for all sorts of things, but it seems we can never get enough to satisfy our cravings. Wouldn't it be nice if there was something so good and filling that it satisfied our cravings and took away the hunger?

Now read what Jesus says in John 6:35: "I am the bread of life. He who comes to me will never go hungry, and he who believes in me will never be thirsty." Talk about what this verse means. How does God take away our hunger?

Other Perspectives   *Help the Hungry.* It's tough to meet peoples' spiritual needs when they have great physical needs. Have your family sponsor a needy child through a development organization

such as Compassion International or World Vision. The letters and monthly support you send to your child provide both kinds of nourishment.

Break Bread. Instead of saying grace before a family meal, take a loaf of bread, break off pieces for everyone, and explain that this bread reminds us of another kind of Bread that keeps us alive: Jesus.

Self-Portraits

When your words came, I ate them;
they were my joy and my heart's delight,
for I bear your name,
O LORD God Almighty.   (Jeremiah 15:16)

And Jesus took bread, gave thanks and broke it, and gave it to them, saying, "This is my body given for you; do this in remembrance of me."   (Luke 22:19)

7 ◆ God Is Like a Carpenter
Work with Wood

Unless the LORD builds the house, its builders labor in vain. (Psalm 127:1)

A carpenter doesn't start a project by swinging a hammer. In fact, that's just about the last thing he does. First he builds the piece in his mind; he decides what it will look like, what materials and tools he'll need. If the design is complicated, he'll then use pencil and paper to sketch out the design and write up a list of materials. Then he gathers the tools and materials together. Finally, he's ready to start swinging the hammer.

God does the same thing with our lives. First He designs us. Next, He gathers up the tools and materials He'll need to make it happen. Then He gets to work.

By the time He shows His project to anyone else (generally on our birthdays), He's already gotten pretty far with the construction. But there's plenty more work to do—walking, talking, learning, growing. To do the job right He uses priceless tools with names like *parent, teacher,* and *friend.*

He starts on the project before you're born, and

He works on it throughout your entire life. He's a perfectionist, and so it takes Him exactly that long to do you right.

Wood Work Build something together with your child—a book stand, birdhouse, doghouse, anything you can make with a minimum of tools. You can get ideas for simple wood projects from a library book. Design the project together. Make a list of tools and materials, and go together to the hardware store.

When you're finished with the project, talk about it: Did the finished piece come out as you expected? What was the toughest part of the job? If you built another one, what would you change?

Now talk about God the Carpenter. Ask your child: "What tools does God use to shape and build you? When God started building you, did He work from a plan? Is He finished with you? If you could look on His design for you, what do you think He wants you to be like in two years? What do you think is the toughest part of the job for Him?"

God has made each of us unique, and He's still working on us. Discuss what God might be doing in your child's life right now. Ask, "Is there anything you can do right now to make God's work easier?"

Other Perspectives *Jesus the Carpenter.*
Watch a carpenter at work. Perhaps his hands are
tough and calloused; his arms may be muscular and
tan. Contrast this image of Jesus as carpenter with
the pictures seen in Sunday school. Ask, "Did Jesus
ever hit His thumb with a hammer? Did He sweat?
Get tired? Feel proud of something He made?"

Self-Portraits

> *You created my inmost being;*
>   *you knit me together in my mother's womb.*
> *I praise you because I am fearfully and*
> *wonderfully made;*
>   *your works are wonderful,*
>   *I know that full well.*
> *My frame was not hidden from you*
>   *when I was made in the secret place.*
> *When I was woven together in the depths of*
> *the earth,*
>   *your eyes saw my unformed body.*
> *All the days ordained for me were written in*
> *your book*
>   *before one of them came to be.*
> (Psalm 139:13–16)

> *Being confident of this, that he who began a*
> *good work in you will carry it on to*
> *completion until the day of Christ*
> *Jesus.*   (Philippians 1:6)

8 ◆ God Is Like a Child

Spy on Preschoolers

Therefore, whoever humbles himself like this child is the greatest in the kingdom of heaven.   (Jesus, Matthew 18:4)

Once upon a time, childhood was when kids could be harmlessly ignorant of adult privileges and vices such as sex, drugs, violence, materialism, and vanity. Not anymore. These "adult" issues and problems are now epidemic among teenagers. And many of the same preoccupations are showing up in elementary schools. Today's kids are growing up way before their time.

When children grow up too fast, they leave behind more than hand-me-downs: they discard a closet filled with beautiful qualities that God intended for them to keep all their lives. Gifts like innocence, lack of prejudice, forgiveness, humor, the ability to play and dream. The tragedy is that these are some of the qualities that make us most like God. Maybe when we start to realize how childlike God is, we'll stop trying to grow up so fast.

Kid Observation   Ask you child to go with you on a scientific journey to study the habits of a strange and fascinating creature. Go to a nearby nursery school (with permission) or a playground and point out the creatures you have come to observe: preschoolers. Sit near the play equipment so you can watch the subjects up close. Mention that some people believe preschoolers have vivid imaginations, are quick to forgive and forget, and are highly skilled at making friends. Your purpose is to look for those kinds of behaviors.

As the two of you point out some of these behaviors, talk about why they're common among small children. For example: Why is it so easy for preschoolers to be angry with someone one minute and best friends with them the next? Why is it tougher for older people to do the same? Why are preschoolers so social? Why don't they seem to care how they look? Why don't adults play and dream as little kids do?

As you observe these and other qualities of childhood, explain that God must be a lot like a child because He has many childlike qualities. Ask her if she can think of stories from the Bible that demonstrate those traits.

Take a moment to express the godly qualities you see in your child. Be sure to give specific examples of times when she demonstrated those qualities so she knows exactly what you mean. When you give her a mental pictures of herself exhibiting those traits, she's less likely to grow out of them as she leaves childhood behind.

Other Perspectives *Photo Flashback.* You can take your child back to her early childhood with photo albums, scrapbooks, and home videos. As the two of you review her past, tell her stories of times when she acted like God the Child.

Jesus the Kid. We don't know a lot about Jesus as a child, but the Bible gives us a few ideas. Read Luke 2:40–52 together and ask your child to describe what she thinks Jesus was like as a kid.

Self-Portraits

> *And [Jesus] said: "I tell you the truth, unless you change and become like little children, you will never enter the kingdom of heaven."*
> (Jesus, Matthew 18:3)

> *"And whoever welcomes a little child like this in my name welcomes me. But if anyone causes one of these little ones who believe in me to sin, it would be better for him to have a large millstone hung around his neck and to be drowned in the depths of the sea."* (Jesus, Matthew 18:5, 6)

9 ◆ God Is Like a Comedian

Host a Comedy Show

Our mouths were filled with laughter, our tongues with songs of joy. (Psalm 126:2)

We don't learn much about God's sense of humor at church; we have to pick it up through our own observations. Imagine for a moment these natural phenomena, and see if you don't come to the same conclusion: monkeys in trees, prairie dogs sunbathing, a duck landing on a lake, a dog chasing its tail, a sea otter doing *anything*.

If the clowns of the animal kingdom don't convince you, observe children doing what comes naturally, like yawning loudly at a boring speech. Or burping in church. Or a baby oozing strained beets out of its mouth—definitely not a learned behavior. Small children know when to laugh, even before we've had a chance to teach them what "funny" means.

Our world is filled with all sorts of funny stuff that humans had nothing to do with. So if we didn't create all this comedy, who did?

Comedy Show   Help your kids put together a comedy show starring themselves. They can do skits, tell jokes, even show a funny video they made up. They can invite their friends to be part of the show or to be the audience.

After all the funny business, have a talk about laughter. Tell of a time you got the giggles when you were supposed to be serious. Ask: "Why do we sometimes laugh the hardest when we shouldn't be laughing at all? Why did God give us laughter? Where do we get a sense of humor? Do you think God likes to watch us laugh? Does God ever laugh?"

Other Perspectives   *Good Fun, Bad Fun.* Sometimes we laugh at another person's expense. Talk about the difference between the fun that builds people up and that which tears them down. Ask your child to come up with examples of each.

Family Jokes.   Pull off fun surprises and jokes for your kids. Throw a birthday party when it is *not* his birthday. Instigate a shaving cream fight while you're washing the car together. Bury a treasure in the yard, and give your child a pirate's map to find it.

10 ◆ God Is Like a Counselor

Hold a Counseling Session

All this also comes from the LORD Almighty, wonderful in counsel and magnificent in wisdom. (Isaiah 28:29)

Many people call themselves counselors: marriage and family counselors, legal counselors, spiritual counselors, camp counselors, career counselors, guidance counselors. While these professions represent a wide variety of disciplines, counselors of any type have share a few things in common. A good counselor in any profession is wise, respected, and knows how to listen and reason.

When the prophet Isaiah predicted Jesus's coming, he said that people would call him Wonderful Counselor. For good reason: Jesus is wiser than anyone on the planet, His excursion down here earned our respect, and He's a whiz at listening to and reasoning with us. Wonderful Counselor.

This is a crazy, complicated world. Without wise counsel, there's no way to see through the confusion and make the right choices. Counselor God is ready to listen, eager to help.

Counseling Session Have your child pretend he's your counselor. Tell him you need his advice about an actual conflict you're having with a friend or coworker. Explain the situation, being sure to describe your *feelings*. For instance, he may not know what it's like to be passed up for a promotion, but he knows what rejection feels like.

When you explain the situation, ask him specific questions about what he thinks you should do. Listen carefully to his answers, and respond with more questions if he's being vague or doesn't seem to understand. The point is to get him to realize the critical responsibility a counselor has. You're counting on him to be a listening ear, to help you see the problem more clearly, and to give you wise advice about what to do.

When the counseling session is over, thank him for his help. Then talk about the job of counselor. Ask: "Have you ever gone to a friend for advice, but, instead of listening, he started telling you what to do before he even heard what your problem was? Have you ever thought of the solution to a problem while explaining the problem to someone else? What makes a good counselor?"

Now talk about Counselor God: "Does God fit the description of a good counselor? Why don't people go to Him with their decisions and problems more often? When you've explained a problem to God, how do you know what advice He's giving you? Is there anything you'd like to talk over with Him now?"

By the way, be sure to follow through on your counseling session by telling your child what you ended up doing about the conflict you discussed. Thank him for helping you clarify your thinking. And if you took his advice, let him know it.

Other Perspectives   *Repeat the Session.*   It's not a bad idea to go to your kids for counsel occasionally. Knowing that you trust and value their opinion is important to them. And you may be surprised at how well they can simplify a confusing problem.

Polish the Mirror.   Kids learn their listening and questioning skills from parents. So if your child is having a tough time with these skills, perhaps you need to work on your own. Each day, sit down for a few minutes with your child. Listen carefully and question thoughtfully.

Self-Portraits

> *To God belong wisdom and power;*
> *   counsel and understanding are*
> his.   (Job 12:13)

11 ◆ God Is Like a Dad

Conduct a Dad Survey

*How great is the love the Father has
lavished on us, that we should be called
children of God! And that is what we
are!* (1 John 3:1)

A little boy's dad took him to a department store
packed with hurried and noisy shoppers. Halfway
down a crowded aisle, the boy got scared and
reached out to take a firm grip of his dad's pant leg.
But when he looked up, the man in the pants wasn't
his dad. It was a stranger, who pulled his leg away
from the boy and walked away. The boy panicked.

Desperately reaching out with the other hand, he
found another pant leg and grasped it with all his
strength. But instead of pulling the cloth from his
grip, this man reached down to pat the boy's head.
The big hand, the smell of the aftershave left no
doubt: this was his dad. He had been walking beside
him the whole time—the boy just didn't know where
to look.

God the Dad walks beside us all the time. As His

sons and daughters, we can reach out and grab His leg. He won't pull away.

Dad Survey   To most kids, dads are dads. They've never really taken the time to analyze the job of being a father. The Dad Survey gives kids a chance to see what constitutes a good dad. Run off several copies of the survey at the end of this section. Have your child call or visit four dads she respects. Ask her to interview these dads by asking them the questions on the survey.

When she's done with all four, talk about the results. Ask: "After hearing what these dads said, what do *you* think are a dad's three most important responsibilities? Why? What did the dads enjoy most about being dads? What were their least favorite parts of being dads?"

Your child can probably think of dads who aren't good dads—maybe even some who beat up on their kids or yell at them too much. She may know kids who don't have dads for one reason or another. Tell her that God knows that some kids have dads they can't hug, or climb on, or cry to. So God has decided to be their dad. In fact, God is everyone's dad, and we're His sons and daughters.

• Like any dad, God doesn't like it when we do bad or selfish things.

- But like a great dad, God doesn't stop loving us when we do.
- Like any dad, God is hurt when we ignore Him or choose to disobey.
- But like a great dad, God never ignores us.

God is a great dad, and He loves His children more than anything else in the whole world.

Other Perspectives *Poster Dad.* A survey may be too difficult for younger children. Instead, give the child a sheet of poster paper and crayons or markers. Have him draw pictures of his dad doing his favorite and least favorite things. Afterward, discuss the pictures and the dad they represent.

Dear Dad Letter.   One way to make praying easier is to have the child write a thank-you note to God the Dad. The letter can start off with Dear Dad; the rest is up to her.

Parable of the Forgiving Dad.   The hero of the story in Luke 15:11–31 is not the prodigal son, but the dad. Read the parable together, and compare that dad to God the Dad.

Dad Survey

What are the 3
most important responsibilities of a dad?

1. _____

2. _____

3. _____

What's your favorite part of being a dad?

_____

_____

_____

What's your *least* favorite thing about being a dad?

_____

_____

_____

12 ◆ God Is Like a Doctor
Visit the Doctor's Office

He heals the brokenhearted and binds up their wounds. (Psalm 147:3)

Doctors can get us to do just about anything.

"Take off your clothes and put on this ridiculous gown."

"Sure."

"Now open your mouth while I jam a Popsicle stick into your throat."

"AHHH."

"I need a sample—fill this cup."

"Where's the bathroom?"

If anyone else told you to do those things, you'd either punch him in the nose or run for your life. So why do we tolerate pain and embarrassment from doctors? Because we trust that they know what's best for us. We believe they have our best interest at heart, and whatever stupid or painful things they make us go through are necessary to make us better and keep us healthy. It's called faith.

Doctor Jesus works the same way. Sometimes He asks us to do things that are painful or embarrassing. We can't figure out why, but we trust that He knows what He's doing, and doing it to make us better.

The Doctor's Office

If your child has a visit with the doctor scheduled soon, turn the appointment into an opportunity to learn about God. On the way to the doctor's office, talk about why you're going. Ask, "Why don't we try to be our own doctor? Why is a trained doctor better? What might happen if you never went to the doctor?"

While you're with the doctor, encourage your child to ask her a few questions, such as: "Why did you choose to be a doctor? What do you like about it? What don't you like? Do you ever have patients who don't do what you tell them? Why don't they do what you say? What happens to them?"

On the way home, talk about the appointment. Ask, "Did the doctor do anything that made you uncomfortable or embarrassed? Did she do anything painful? Why did you do as you were told? Can you think of ways that God is like a doctor? Does He ever ask you to do things that are embarrassing or painful? Does He always take away your pain? Can you think of an example when physical pain could be a good thing? How about emotional pain—rejection, heartbreak, failure—why does God let us suffer?"

Wrap up the conversation by asking your child if

she can think of anything Doctor God is asking her to do to make her healthier. "Is there some lesson He's teaching right now? Are you going through any kind of trial or emotional pain that God can use to strengthen you? How can that experience make you better? What can you do right now to learn from the pain?"

Other Perspectives *Meet Someone Who's Been Healed.* Talk together with someone who's come through a major emotional or physical trauma such as an addiction, divorce, severe injury, or a long-term illness. Ask the person what part God plays in the healing process. Did he doubt God's love, intentions, or existence? In what ways is life better now?

Trial Advice. Read James 1:2–12 together and try to figure out what James was saying about the benefits of trials. Is it really possible to consider them good? What's the reward for withstanding them?

Self-Portraits

> *O LORD my God, I called to you for help and you healed me.* (Psalm 30:2)

13 ◆ God Is Like a Dreamer

Daydream Together

Delight yourself in the LORD and he will give you the desires of your heart. Commit your way to the LORD; trust in him and he will do this. (Psalm 37:4, 5)

Some of humankind's biggest accomplishments started out as dreams. What if there was a "back road" to China? Hello America. What if man could fly? Try an airplane. What if there was a vaccine for polio? Dr. Salk pursued the dream.

Dreaming is a beautiful gift given to us by a God who dreamed the universe into existence. It's a priceless gift in an imperfect world. In a perfect world, *what is* is the best it can be. There's no need to ask *what if?* when it's impossible to imagine something better.

But our world is far from perfect. You *can* imagine a better world and even entertain the thought of trying to get there. You can dream. You can ask *what if?*

Sometimes God the Dreamer plants His dream in the hearts of His people. The Israelites dreamed of the "promised land," so wonderful it flowed with milk and honey. They dreamed of a temple of God in

Jerusalem. They dreamed of a Messiah. God fulfilled those dreams through His people.

The good news is God still dreams, and He plants His dreams in our hearts. Our job is to take a look inside to discover the dreams He's given us to fulfill.

Brainstorm   Little kids dream and imagine constantly. But somewhere along the way to adulthood they cut down on asking *what if?* and get preoccupied with *what is.* You can help them hold onto this precious gift by dreaming with them. Here are a few brainstorm sessions you and your child can try:

- What if you decided to build a new house for your family? Money is no object. What does it look like? Does it have an indoor pool? Are there water slides from every bedroom? How about a rope swing from your room to the kitchen—in case you're hungry for a banana in the middle of the night? Does the garage convert to a drive-in theater? You get the idea. Sketch your dream house on paper, interview family members about what they'd like.
- What if the school board asked you to design a new school, hire new teachers, change the classroom size, come up with new subjects? What does the new school look like? How many students are in each class? What are the teachers like? What happens when the teacher sends kids

to the office? What subjects are taught at the
school?

- What if you decided to build an amusement park
in your neighborhood? What are the rides like?
Describe one of the roller coasters.
- What if you were elected President? What
things would you change?
- What if you decided to cure a disease? Which
one would you work on? How would you figure
out the cure? What effect would your accom-
plishment have on others?

After your brainstorm session, talk about God the
Dreamer. Did God do a similar thing when He decided to create the world? Does God still dream?
What are some of His dreams now? Are they idle
dreams, or does He work on making them come
true? How does God make His dreams come true?

Mention some examples of people who dreamed
for God and had their dreams come true: Joshua and
Jericho, David with Goliath (Fight Goliath?!—dream
on, David!), Daniel in Babylon, Nehemiah rebuilding
Jerusalem. "How do you dream for God? Do you
have dreams right now that might be part of God's
dreams too? How can God help you make them come
true?"

14 ♦ God Is Like an Eagle

Study Eagles

. . . he guarded him as the apple of his eye, like an eagle that stirs up its nest and hovers over its young, that spreads its wings to catch them and carries them on its pinions.   (Deuteronomy 32:10, 11)

The great moment in an eagle's life is when it learns to fly. There are no classroom lessons, textbooks, films, lectures, or homework. The mother just transports the eaglet on her wings to a high altitude and lets it fall—a crash course, as it were.

Well, not quite. She swoops down and catches the child before the course is over. Then she repeats the lesson until the eaglet gets the hang of it. With each test flight the child's wings grow stronger. It learns balance and flight control, and how to soar inside columns of rising air. Eventually it learns to take off, fly, and land on its own. Another eagle earns its wings.

God the Eagle does the same thing to us. Sometimes He drops us into unfamiliar and frightening situations. We learn to fly by faith, faith that He knows what He's doing; that He loves us so much He won't allow us to be destroyed; that flying will be so incredible that it's worth all He's putting us through to learn.

Eagle Study   Read a book together about eagles. Talk about how they take care of their young, learn to fly, how they soar. Ask your child to imagine what it would be like to learn to fly that way. "What would you be thinking as your mother let you go? Would you think she was trying to kill you? Why does she teach flying this way? Does *she* ever get scared for her child?"

Now talk about God the Eagle. Sometimes God introduces us to new ways of thinking or acting by putting us in new situations where we learn out of necessity. Ask your child to think of examples? Has he ever been scared that God wouldn't catch him?

Self-Portraits

> *You yourselves have seen what I did to Egypt, and how I carried you on eagles' wings and brought you to myself.*   (Exodus 19:4)

> *But those who hope in the LORD*
> *   will renew their strength.*
> *They will soar on wings like eagles;*
> *   they will run and not grow weary,*
> *   they will walk and not be faint.*
> (Isaiah 40:31)

15 ◆ God Is Like a Fire

Burn Something

*. . . for our God is a consuming
fire.* (Hebrews 12:29)

As a child I learned a lot about life by sitting next to a
fire at summer camp. My friends and I would argue
and criticize and joke the entire day, but as soon as
we sat around the campfire, our conversation
changed. What we said around the fire was deep—
deeply funny, deeply serious, deeply moving, and
now rooted deep in my memory. It was as if the fire
reached inside us and drew out thoughts and feelings
we didn't even know we had.

God was a frequent topic around those fires.
Maybe the mystery of fire made us contemplate the
mystery of God. Or maybe it was the warmth of the
fire that spurred our conversations. Ten feet away
from the fire, the air was as cold as if there was no
fire. Three feet away and you were comfortable and
warm. Move one foot closer and it singed the hair on
your arms.

God is like a fire. He brings warmth and lights up
the darkest places in our lives. He thaws out our
hearts until we begin to feel things inside we didn't

know were there. If we move too far away from God, we feel cold and alone. Get close, and we are glad to be counted among His friends instead of His enemies.

Build a Fire   You don't have to go to summer camp to have a campfire. Find a park or beach where campfires are allowed. Bring firewood, kindling, paper, matches, and some marshmallows.

After roasting marshmallows, ask your child, "Why do people enjoy sitting around a fire? What would life be like without fire? What's your favorite thing about a fire? What happens if you get too careless with a fire? What happens when you get too far away?"

Now steer the conversation toward God. Explain that the Bible says God is like a fire. Ask, "Do you think that's true? In what ways? If God is like a fire, how can we be sure to stay warm? Does God ever burn people? How? What can you do to keep from getting burned? What happens when you move too far away from God? How can you prevent that from happening?"

Other Perspectives *Homemade Fire.* If building an outdoor fire isn't possible, you can use a fireplace. Make the activity special by allowing your child to stay up past bedtime to enjoy the fire with you.

16 ◆ God Is Like a Fort

Take a Fort Tour

The LORD is a refuge for the oppressed, a stronghold in times of trouble. (Psalm 9:9)

Every kid builds forts, though not every kid calls it a fort. Sometimes the "fort" is called a spaceship, pirate ship, treehouse, hideout, or playhouse.

My nephew Brice builds couch forts—sofa cushions and blankets carefully arranged to form a fortress in the living room. He also makes forts from cardboard boxes, trash cans, and anything else he can find on the side of the house. He builds his forts to protect himself from all sorts of hazards, including naptime and an over-exuberant dog that tries to lick his face off. Soon he'll graduate to a fort made from wood and carpet scraps, stuck in a tree or gully near his house. I'm sure it will have a skull-and-crossbones drawn on the door.

When he grows out of that one, he'll convert his room into a fort. It will be plush as fortresses go, complete with stereo, maybe a phone, and wall-to-wall piles of games, sports equipment, and clothes. The sign on the door will say "Trespassers will be eaten!" After that, he'll get a *moving* fort—a car. This time the sign will be on the license plate frame —"If you don't like the way I drive, stay off the sidewalk."

Why all these forts? Why do we have this need to establish hiding places we can call our own? Instinctively we seem to know that the world can be a dangerous place. I think we build strongholds where we can feel safe from the scary things in life.

God is like a fort. We can run to Him when we're overwhelmed by the world's troubles and fears. We can escape to the fort of God's presence.

Fort Tour   Ask your child for a tour of his secret hiding place. If he doesn't have one at the moment, build a fort together. Sit together in the fort and talk about what makes forts so special. Ask, "Why do kids like to build forts? What do you think about when you're sitting in yours?"

Talk about how people throughout history used fortresses to protect themselves from attacking enemies. When an enemy army swept into a village, the people would run for the fortress to save their lives. The gates would be locked, the doors closed, and the people would be safe from their enemies.

Now explain how God is like a fort. When you're scared and being chased by enemies, you can take your heart to him and he keeps it safe. Close the discussion by assuring your child that God promises to be the fort for his heart. When he's in pain or frightened by anything, he can run to God, call out for help, and God will open up the fortress gates and hide his heart inside.

Other Perspectives   *Room Forts.*   For lots of kids, especially older ones, their bedroom is their refuge. Ask if you can take a tour. Have your child explain what is on the walls and shelves, and why. Ask what he likes most and least about his room.

Self-Portraits

> *You are my hiding place;*
> *   you will protect me from trouble*
> *   and surround me with songs of*
> *deliverance.*   (Psalm 32:7)

> *But I will sing of your strength,*
> *   in the morning I will sing of your love;*
> *for you are my fortress,*
> *   my refuge in times of trouble.*
> (Psalm 59:16)

> *I will say of the* LORD, *"He is my refuge and my fortress,*
> *my God, in whom I trust."*   (Psalm 91:2)

17 ◆ God Is Like a Foundation
Build a Wall

See, I lay a stone in Zion, a tested stone, a precious cornerstone for a sure foundation; the one who trusts will never be dismayed. (Isaiah 28:16)

With most things in life, if you get off to a rough start you can go back and fix the problem later. If you don't like the introduction to a story you're writing, you can finish the story and then go back and rewrite the opening. If you get a bad grade on the first test in a class, you can still pull off a high grade by doing well on other tests.

But when it comes to building a stone wall, if you don't set that first stone straight, everything above it will always be crooked or unstable no matter how you try to compensate. Tearing down the wall and starting over is the only option.

God wants us to build our lives on a firm and straight foundation.

Build a Wall Build a wall with your child using blocks, bricks, boxes, books—anything you can stack. Start the activity by building the wall on something unstable—crooked ground, crumpled up newspapers, lumpy pillows. The wall is okay for the first course or two, but then it becomes obvious that the structure is crooked and getting worse the higher you go.

Knock down this wall and start over. This time build upon flat, solid ground. Compare the stability of the two walls. Now talk with your child about the importance of a solid foundation. Explain that the world is a big and wild place, with lots of people offering answers to anyone who will listen. God says we need to believe something solid and true, or we'll fall apart when tough times come. Talk about the foundation God has in mind for our lives.

Self-Portraits

> *God's household [is] built on the foundation of the apostles and prophets, with Christ Jesus himself as the chief cornerstone.*   (Ephesians 2:20)

> *For in Scripture it says: "See, I lay a stone in Zion,*
> *a chosen and precious cornerstone,*
> *and the one who trusts in him*
> *will never be put to shame."*
> (1 Peter 2:6)

18 ◆ God Is Like a Genius

Take a Trivia Quiz

Among all the wise men of the nations and in all their kingdoms, there is no one like you.   (Jeremiah 10:7)

God knows everything, including answers to age-old questions such as . . .

- How many angels *can* dance on the head of a pin?
- Can God make a rock so heavy he can't lift it?
- How high is up?

And he knows a few other things, like the number of hairs on your head. The names and addresses of everyone you've ever cut in front of on the freeway. He knows the number of calories in a Hershey's Kiss the size of Kilimanjaro. He knows the birthdates of all your family's pets clear back through the ages starting with the day your distant Uncle Ug discovered a litter of saber-toothed tigers in the back of his cave.

God knows all your problems, including the ones you won't admit to (and a dozen more you don't even know you have). God the Genius knows about your biggest dreams, your worst fears. He's the only one who knows that you still check under your bed for the bogeyman. He knows the best answer to your toughest dilemmas.

What's more amazing than how much God knows? How little we ask Him for the answers. Look at it this way. Here's someone who knows *everything,* and most of us don't bother to ask Him for advice. Yet he's been known to share His knowledge with those who really desire it.

M&M's Candy Quiz   Play a game with your child using questions from a trivia book or the cards from a trivia game. Set a bowl of M&M's candy on the table. For every simple question answered correctly, take one candy; tougher questions are worth two candies, and the toughest questions pay three. Alternate asking and being asked; play until the candies are gone.

After the game, talk about how smart God is. There isn't a question in the world that God can't answer. Ask, "What are some things that would be impossible for humans to know (number of grains of sand on the beach, number of stars in the sky, why God allows good people to die, what heaven is like)? If God is a genius, why doesn't He share all His knowledge with us? Does He share *any* of it? How?"

19 ◆ God Is Like a Gift

Open a Present

For it is by grace you have been saved, through faith—and this not from yourselves, it is the gift of God. (Ephesians 2:8)

You can't earn God—He's a gift. Wouldn't He *have* to be? Can you imagine earning Him by, let's say, selling magazine subscriptions through the school's fund-raising drive? You have to sell ten subscriptions to earn a nifty pen-and-pencil set and 50 to get a Walkman. At that rate, how many would it take earn the Creator of the universe?

You can't redeem your frequent flyer miles for Him, nor can you win Him with a lottery ticket. You can't buy, lease, rent, earn, or win Him. He's a gift: you take it, open it, and say thank you.

Open a Present   Buy and wrap a gift your child would enjoy. Put a tag on it with his name, but don't write who it's from.

Walk in the room with the gift and announce that you found it at the door. Here's how the ensuing conversation might go:

MOM   Hey, look what I found at the front door.

SON   Who's it for?

MOM   The tag says it's for you.

SON   Great! Let me have it.

MOM   Hold on. Maybe it's a birthday gift you shouldn't open until then.

SON   My birthday isn't for three more months!

MOM   You can wait that long.

SON   No way!

MOM   Well, maybe it's a Christmas present.

SON   Right! I can't wait all year! Please let me have it.

MOM   Well, I'm not even sure it's for you. Maybe it's for someone else with the same name. Wouldn't it be horrible if you opened someone else's gift by mistake.

SON   Mom! Let me open it!

MOM   (shaking it) Hmm . . . I wonder what it is?

SON   Mom!

MOM   I'll give it to you in a minute, but first let me tell you something. I'm the one who got you this gift. I didn't get it for any reason except that you're my son and I love you. You didn't earn it. I'm not giving it to you as a reward for good grades, or because you cleaned your room, or because you were nice to your little sister. Believe it or not, if you hadn't done those things, I still would give you this gift.

Give the child the gift, and let him open it. Afterwards, explain to him that God has given us Himself as a gift. Some people try to earn God's love. They figure that if they do enough nice things, or go to church every week, or give money to charity, God will decide to love them. But God is priceless. No one can afford to buy Him. God's love is a gift. There's nothing you can do but take it, open it, and thank Him for it.

Self-Portraits

> *For the wages of sin is death, but the gift of God is eternal life in Christ Jesus our Lord.*   (Romans 6:23)

> *Thanks be to God for his indescribable gift!*   (2 Corinthians 9:15)

> *Every good and perfect gift is from above, coming down from the Father of the heavenly lights, who does not change like shifting shadows.*   (James 1:17)

> *Each one should use whatever gift he has received to serve others, faithfully administering God's grace in its various forms.*   (1 Peter 4:10)

20 ◆ God Is Like a Guide
Take a Trust Walk

I will lead the blind by ways they have not known, along unfamiliar paths I will guide them; I will turn the darkness into light before them and make the rough places smooth. (Isaiah 42:16)

Life is a jungle. It's full of beautiful sights, exciting adventures, and wonderfully friendly natives. But it's also dangerous—wild animals, deadly situations, and a few *un*friendly natives. If you want to experience the best that life has to offer, you need someone who knows the territory, someone who can take you to the best parts of the jungle while guiding you safely through the dangers. You need a guide.

Jesus is like a guide. He knows His way through life's jungle better than anyone. He wants to show you His favorite sights, places you could never find on your own. Getting to those places means passing through some pretty tough parts of the jungle, but He's an excellent guide and those who stick close to Him can make it past the dangers.

Trust Walk   Lead your child on a trust walk. You do this by blindfolding her and then leading her by the arm. Because she can't see, she has to rely on your guidance to keep her from falling or bumping into things. After several minutes of this, switch places and let her guide you.

Afterwards, talk about the experience: Ask, "How did you feel? Were you frightened? Did following get easier as time went on?" Then talk about Jesus: "How does Jesus act as a guide? Why can you trust Him? Why should you follow Him as your guide? If you follow Jesus the Guide, will you ever run into trouble? How can you learn to trust Him more as your guide?"

Self-Portraits

> *For this God is our God for ever and ever;*
> *he will be our guide even to the end.*
> (Psalm 48:14)

> *I guide you in the way of wisdom*
> *and lead you along straight paths.*
> *When you walk, your steps will not be*
> *hampered; when you run, you will not*
> *stumble.*   (Proverbs 4:12)

21 ◆ God Is Like an Heir

Make a Will

. . . but in these last days he has spoken to us by his Son, whom he appointed heir of all things, and through whom he made the universe. (Hebrews 1:2)

In one sense, giving your life to Jesus is like putting Him in your will. When you die, others may get your *stuff*—house, car, lawn mower, Beatles albums—but He gets *you*. And He's thrilled! He finally gets to take you home to be with Him forever. God doesn't *have* to claim His inheritance—He *chooses* to accept you.

Paul puts it this way in Ephesians 1:18: "I pray also that the eyes of your heart may be enlightened in order that you may know the hope to which He has called you, *the riches of His glorious inheritance* in the saints . . . [my italics]." God inherits *you*—and He considers it *rich and glorious*.

Make a Will Help your child write a will. It doesn't have to be official, just a list of possessions and who the child would like to give them to. Let the last beneficiary be God, and the bequest is the child's eternal life. Explain: "When you become a follower of

Jesus, you give yourself to Him. When you die, He gets what is left—your soul."

Ask: "Why does God want to inherit us?"

Self-Portraits

> *The* LORD *will inherit Judah as his portion in the holy land and will again choose Jerusalem.*   (Zechariah 2:12)

> *So he became as much superior to the angels as the name he has inherited is superior to theirs.*   (Hebrews 1:4)

22 ◆ God Is Like a Hen

(Try to) Pet a Chicken

. . . how often I have longed to gather your children together, as a hen gathers her chicks under her wings, but you were not willing! (Jesus, Luke 13:34)

Wait a minute: God is like a *hen?*

But isn't a hen a female chicken? Isn't chicken the main ingredient in McNuggets, and isn't "Chicken!" an expression used to describe a coward? Isn't the chicken the butt of all jokes pertaining to crossing a particular road? And do they, or do they not, have heads that bob like something that belongs in the back window of a '65 Impala? All true, but that's not the whole story.

The moment you threaten a hen's chicks, this humble bird with the bobbing head and silly walk is transformed into a storm of wings and feathers, riveting beak, scratching claws, and ear-shattering squawking. If she succeeds in stopping your invasion, she gathers her chicks about her and spreads her wings in protection. The message is clear: if you want one of her chicks, you'll have to go through her to get it. And that's a good picture of how God protects us.

Try to Pet a Chicken   Visit a petting zoo or a farm with free-range chickens. Together with your child, watch how a hen looks after her chicks. Carefully approach her chicks to see the hen's reaction. She's not as worried about you as she is of a cat or dog, so she probably won't fly into a rage as she would with a more natural predator. If hens with chicks aren't available, observe any mother animal with her young.

Talk about what you've seen. Ask your child: "Do the chicks feel safer knowing their mom is watching over them? Do you think they're ever tired of having her be so protective? How can she be so angry with us for trying to get one of her children, and yet so loving toward her chicks?"

Talk about God the Hen. Ask your child to compare the hen to God: "How are God and the hen alike? Does God get angry with those who try to harm us? How does God cover us with His wings? Have you ever felt Him do that? How did it feel?"

Other Perspectives   *Seek Shade.*   Go for a walk on a hot day. When the heat becomes uncomfortable, sit in the shadow of a tree. Talk about the importance of shade. Ask, "How can shade protect us (from sunburn, dehydration, heat, exhaustion, en-

emy eyes)?" Then talk about the shadow of God's wings. Ask, "How does God protect us from danger?"

Self-Portraits

How priceless is your unfailing love!
Both high and low among men
   find refuge in the shadow of your
wings.   (Psalm 36:7)

Have mercy on me, O God, have mercy on
me,
   for in you my soul takes refuge.
I will take refuge in the shadow of your
wings
   until the disaster has passed.
(Psalm 57:1)

He will cover you with his feathers,
   and under his wings you will find refuge;
his faithfulness will be your shield and
rampart.   (Psalm 91:4)

23 ◆ God Is Like a Human

Go Back in Time

The Word became flesh and lived for a while among us. (John 1:14)

As a real, live human being, Jesus got to experience the joys of humanity first hand: laughter, sunsets, back rubs, dinner with dessert, late-night conversations with friends around a fire; the way the air smells after rain.

But Jesus also got to taste the bitter stuff: diaper rash, stubbed toes, smashed thumbs, splinters under the fingernail, boring teachers, rejection from friends, loneliness, hatred, temptation, wicked people, hunger, thirst, murder. He's not some distant and unknowable Force who's so different from us that He can't relate. He's eaten, laughed, cried, and bled—just like you. He's been in your shoes; He *knows* what it's like.

Flashback Children sometimes have a tough time imagining that parents were ever their age. Solution: prove that you were. Find evidence of your childhood in scrapbooks, photo albums, and keepsake boxes. Ask your child to join you for a trip into your past.

Instead of focusing on what you did at their age, try to describe how you felt, what you thought, what the world looked like to you back then. For example, when you show him your team picture from Little League, describe how you felt when you struck out in the playoffs—how bad you hurt inside, how you cried all the way home. Share your moments of triumph—what you felt, how they changed your perspective. Talk about when you messed up, when you got angry or sad.

Ask your child if he's ever felt those same feelings, and when. The goal is to reverse the empathy process. Usually you say, "Son, I know how you feel"; here you want your son to say (silently or aloud), "Dad, I know how you felt." Empathy and intimacy feed each other: understanding begets closeness, closeness begets understanding.

Now talk about Jesus. If Jesus could show us His scrapbook and photo album, He'd show pictures and tell stories of things He did and felt, and we'd say, "Wow! I know how You felt." Jesus would listen to our stories and say the same thing. Ask your child: "What are some of the frustrations Jesus had? How do you think He felt? How about His triumphs? How did those feel? Have you ever had a feeling that He couldn't relate to?"

Other Perspectives   *Grandmother Tells All.*
Let your child interview your parents or siblings
about what you were like as a kid. They'll volunteer
stories you might not tell yourself, but you'll look a
lot more human to your kid once he hears them.

Self-Portraits

> *For we do not have a high priest who is*
> *unable to sympathize with our weaknesses,*
> *but we have one who has been tempted in*
> *every way, just as we are—yet was without*
> *sin. Let us then approach the throne of grace*
> *with confidence, so that we may receive mercy*
> *and find grace to help us in our time of*
> *need.*   (Hebrews 4:15, 16)

24 ◆ God Is Like an Inventor
Make a Miniature World

You made the heavens, even the highest heavens, and all their starry host, the earth and all that is on it, the seas and all that is in them. (Nehemiah 9:6)

Have you ever created a world? A hundred times. As a child you created worlds with tinker toys, troll dolls, and Tonka trucks. You invented towns and countries in your mind and then built them with blocks, Lego blocks, and Lincoln Logs. You inherited this knack for creating stuff from your Father, who's best known for inventing the universe.

Make a World You can help your child get in touch with the inventive side of God by inventing your own world together. Set it up like this: God is forming a planet on the other side of the universe, and He wants the two of you to name the planet and design it for Him. Right now it's completely covered with water—you have to tell him where to put the land. It's smaller than earth, with enough room for three or four small continents.

Draw two large circles on poster board to represent the two hemispheres. Now decide where to put the continents. Draw their shapes and name them. Add islands if you like. Then, using assorted colored pens, create the geography: indicate mountains, deserts, plains, rivers, lakes—whatever you want. Decide on political borders: Is there just one government or several countries? Draw the borders, give names to the countries. Now decide where the people will live. Where are the cities, towns, and farmlands?

You can stop there or continue by inventing the kinds of plants and animals that live there, the climates and seasons, and what the people look like. When you're finished, talk about the experience. Was it fun? Hard? Ask, "How would you feel if the people who live on your planet started messing up all your work—killing off the animals, spoiling rivers, cutting down all the forests?"

Talk about God the Inventor: "Do you think God had fun when He created the universe? How did He decide what went where? Do you think it bothers Him when we mess up His invention? How does it make Him feel? Does He want us to be inventors like Him, or does He prefer us to leave things as they are?

Self-Portraits

But ask the animals, and they will teach you,
*   or the birds of the air, and they will tell*
you;
*   or speak to the earth, and it will teach you,*
*   or let the fish of the sea inform you.*
Which of all these does not know
*   that the hand of the LORD has done*
this?   (Job 12:7–9)

The earth is the LORD'S, and everything in it,
*   the world, and all who live in it;*
for he founded it upon the seas
*   and established it upon the*
waters.   (Psalm 24:1, 2)

In the beginning you laid the foundations of
the earth,
*   and the heavens are the work of your*
hands.   (Psalm 102:25)

For every house is built by someone, but God
is the builder of everything.
(Hebrews 3:4)

25 ◆ God Is Like a Jealous Lover
Read a Love Story

Do not worship any other god, for the LORD, whose name is Jealous, is a jealous God. (Exodus 34:14)

The book of Hosea is a love story. At first you think it's just about a guy named Hosea, a girl named Gomer, and the children she bore—Jezreel, Lo-Ruhamah, and Lo-Ammi (you can imagine *their* first day at school). But then you realize it's also a love story about a guy named God, a girl named Israel, and the children *she* bore—Sin, Rebellion, and Unfaithfulness.

God is a jealous lover. He hates it when we set Him aside to pursue other loves. After all, He's sworn himself to be *our* lover—He's made no secret promises to potatoes or parakeets. As our lover, He's chosen to carry out His dreams through us. If we intend to be faithful, we've got to live our dreams through Him.

Read about Love Read the first three chapters of the book of Hosea together. It's not quite like a modern romance novel. It's well-written for one thing, and much shorter for another. When you're finished, talk about the first love story—Hosea and Gomer: "Why was Hosea jealous? What did he do about it? Why did Gomer leave Hosea to love other men? Do you think she felt bad about it? Did she think about how it was hurting Hosea? What made Hosea take Gomer back?"

Then talk about the second love story—God and Israel: "Why did God get jealous? What did he do about it? Why did Israel abandon God? What made God take Israel back?"

Now talk about God's jealous love for us: "What things could you do that might make God jealous? Why would he be jealous? How does it make you feel to know that God loves you so much he can't stand it when you don't put him first?"

Self-Portraits

> *You shall not bow down to them or worship them; for I, the LORD your God, am a jealous God, punishing the children for the sin of the fathers to the third and fourth generation of those who hate me.*   (Exodus 20:5)

> *For the LORD your God is a consuming fire, a jealous God.*   (Deuteronomy 4:24)

26 ◆ God Is Like a Judge
Go to Court

And the heavens proclaim his righteousness, for God himself is judge. (Psalm 50:6)

You hear a lot about justice from your kids, at least as it applies to how others treat them. It's *me*-justice: *I* didn't do it, *I* don't deserve it, it's not fair for *me*. The Bible talks about justice too, but mostly it's *you*-justice—the kind you do for others. Judges are commissioned to administer this kind of justice. Their job is to sift out the grains of truth from the sandstorm of fiction, exaggeration, and half-truth, and then do the fair thing, no matter how painful it is.

Getting to the truth is no simple task. Thanks to God's habit of making us all unique, any two people witnessing the same occurrence are bound to see it differently. So a courtroom judge has to hear everyone describe her version and then try to imagine what *really* happened. One of the reasons why Judge God is so fair is that He doesn't have to rely on the testimony of witnesses. He sees everything and therefore knows all the facts. He also sees what's in our hearts, and so He knows the motive behind every action. He knows the truth and judges us accordingly.

Court Date   You can help your child see God as a fair judge by taking him to a courtroom. Jury trials are seldom as exciting as they're portrayed on TV (unless *you're* the one being tried), but if you check the docket at the courthouse you may be able to catch part of a felony trial. Stay long enough to point out the various characters in the drama, to see a witness being sworn in, and to watch how the judge directs the proceedings.

Outside the courtroom, talk with your child about the role of a judge. Ask, "Why do people stand when she enters the room? Why does she wear a robe and sit higher than everyone else? Why do people address her *honor* rather than *her?* How does she know people are telling the truth? Do you think she feels sorry for people? Does she feel bad when she sentences someone to prison? If you were on trial for something, what kind of judge would you want?"

Now talk about Judge God: "How does He know when people are telling the truth? Does God treat people unfairly?"

Other Perspectives *The Honorable Judge God, Presiding.* Encourage your child to "approach the bench"—to stand before the Judge and tell Him her story. Read together 1 John 1:9: "If we confess our sins, he is faithful and just and will forgive us our sins and purify us from all unrighteousness."

Act Justly. Micah 6:8 tells us "to act justly." Ask your child to think of a circumstance where someone wasn't treated justly (e.g., blamed for something he didn't do, denied the chance to defend himself). Who or what stood in the way of justice? Is there something your child could do to help justice prevail the next time that kind of situation occurs?

Self-Portraits

> *Now let the fear of the LORD be upon you.*
> *Judge carefully, for with the LORD our God*
> *there is no injustice or partiality or*
> *bribery.*   (2 Chronicles 19:7)

> *The Almighty is beyond our reach and*
> *exalted in power;*
> *   in his justice and great righteousness,*
> *He does not oppress.*   (Job 37:23)

27 ◆ God Is Like a King
Hold a Coronation

I am the Lord, your Holy One, Israel's Creator, your King.   (Isaiah 43:15)

If as a child you were ever left in the care of an older sibling, you know what it's like to be ruled by a king or queen. The rules of monarchy are simple:

- The king owns everything in the kingdom.
- If he lets you have anything, it's a favor, not a right.
- If the king tells you to do something and you refuse, he can have your head.

These rules sound oppressive to those of us raised on the promises of life, liberty and the pursuit of happiness, yet they were the principles of virtually all governments worldwide a couple hundred years ago (and the status quo in a few countries to this day). The characteristics of a monarchy are important in understanding how God rules the world. God is not the President of Presidents, Prime Minister Eternal, or Chairman of the Universe. He's King. Which means:

- King God owns everything. He is the landlord, the master, the owner.
- King God lets us use His possessions on His behalf. We are God's slaves, stewards, servants, and one day we'll be called to account for what we did with them.
- If King God tells us to do something and we refuse, He can punish us as rebellious subjects.

What makes God a *good* king is how He treats His subjects. He's wise, generous, just, merciful, protective, quick to listen, slow to anger, and takes His greatest pleasure in seeing us happy. He loves us so much He's adopted us as His sons and daughters so we can live in His palace forever. Hail the King!

King for an Evening   To let your child understand what King God is like, crown him king (or her, queen) of your house for one evening. Make a paper crown with his name on it, give him a broom handle for a scepter. Explain that he's the ruler of the house and the family are his subjects: he's to decide about dinner, who's to prepare it, the evening entertainment, and so on. (You may want to explain that his siblings will get their moment in the throne on subsequent evenings, and so he'll get to taste his own tyranny if he gets too mean.) Set a time when the crown comes off and the family returns to "parent rule."

When your child's reign is over, talk about how he

felt being king. Was it fun? Difficult? Was he tempted to take advantage of his subjects? What qualities make for a good subject? How does a king keep his subjects happy? What are the differences between a good king and a bad one?

Now talk about King God: Ask, "How is God king of the universe? Is He a good king? In what ways? How are you doing as His subject? What's something you can be doing now to be a better subject?"

Self-Portraits

The LORD will reign for ever and
ever.   (Exodus 15:18)

How awesome is the LORD Most High,
    the great King over all the earth! He
subdued nations under us,
    peoples under our feet.   (Psalm 47:2, 3)

Now to the King eternal, immortal, invisible,
the only God, be honor and glory for ever and
ever. Amen   (1 Timothy 1:17).

28 ◆ God Is Like a Lamb

Sacrifice Something

*Look, the Lamb of God, who takes away
the sin of the world!*   (John 1:29)

The Jews were told by God to take animals of great
value and kill them to "pay" for their sins. This re-
minded them that sin was "expensive"—it hurt God
deeply, and stood in the way of making Israel a great
and powerful nation. Animal sacrifice also showed
them how filthy and wasteful sin was because the
sacrifice required wasting a beautiful and innocent
life to cover the selfishness of the guilty.

God was very specific about the types of animals
He wanted for payment. He wouldn't allow people to
offer up their "discards"—old or lame animals that
had little value—He was God Almighty, not a beggar
in the street. One of the most expensive sacrifices
they had to make was that of a year-old lamb with no
marks or defects. This meant that they'd have to
watch carefully over the best lambs and, just when
these perfect lambs were getting old enough to earn
their keep in meat, wool, or breeding, give them to
God. Doing so was a real sacrifice.

In the same way, Jesus was a sacrificial lamb: a

beautiful and innocent life taken to pay for our self-ishness. It was a sacrifice so expensive, God was the only one who could afford the price (hence, Lamb of *God)*—and the payment killed him. It was a sacrifice so perfect that it covered the payment on all sins that would ever be committed throughout time. Which is good news for year-old lambs, and *great* news for humans of all ages.

Sacrifice   Help your child understand the nature of God's sacrifice by encouraging him to make a sacrifice himself. Tell him you'd like to make a pile of stuff to donate to an organization such as the Salvation Army, first by helping him pick out stuff in his room and then by having him help you pick out stuff from yours. Together go through his closet, shelves, and drawers and pull out all the clothing, toys, and games he no longer needs.

When you've finished making his donation pile, say something like this: "It's great that you're willing to donate this stuff because they work with families who can't afford new clothes and toys, and this will really help them. But it's also doing *you* a favor because you don't have much use for the stuff anymore; it was just taking up space. A real sacrifice is painful because it means giving up something of great value to you. I'd like to see you make that kind of a sacrifice. I'll help you make it, and then we can go in and do the same thing with my things. Do you think you can do it?"

Help him pick one of his favorite possessions to put on the donation pile. It's important that you not force him to do it—you don't want to embitter him toward the idea of giving. If he firmly refuses, just move on to your room. If he picks out something to give, ask him what he likes about the item and why it's so hard to give up. Thank him for doing it, then head over to your room and start over.

When you're done with your donations and sacrificial gift, pack it all up and take it right to the donation facility. On the way back, stop for ice cream and talk about Jesus the Lamb and his sacrifice of the most precious thing he had: Why did Jesus die?

29 ◆ God Is Like Life

Visit a Cemetery

I am the resurrection and the life. He who believes in me will live even though he dies. (Jesus, John 11:25)

A man had a dream. He's standing in a dark room when a figure appears and starts walking toward him. As the figure gets closer, he recognizes it: Death. There's no face, just a black, hooded cloak, and in Death's hand is a sickle.

Fear paralyzes the man: he can't run away, can't scream for help; he can barely even breath. Death stops and points. The man is certain: "He's come for *me.*" Death raises the sickle, then swings. But before the blade touches the man, it's blocked by someone else's body. This person, whoever he is, falls dead. Death covers the face with a shroud. Then he turns and walks away. The man shouts, "Where are you going?! You came for me!" But Death doesn't even turn around; in a moment he's gone.

The man kneels at the body of the person who took Death's blow. He lifts the shroud. He looks into the face of a man he'd never met. He replaces the shroud and steps back from the body, feeling sick and

confused. There comes a shudder from the corpse;
then it sits up, then stands, then pulls the shroud
from its face, like a statue making its own unveiling.
But it's not a statue—the man is alive. He tears the
shroud in half and tosses the shreds aside. His face is
brilliant. The blood is gone; his shirt is blinding white,
a scar marks his neck. He smiles and walks away.

You guessed it—this wasn't a dream. It's an alle-
gory of what actually happened to *you*. You're the one
Death came for. You're the one Death swung at. But
Jesus stepped in and took your place. He took your
death and died for you. It's like he stole the period
from the end of your sentence And he put it in the .
middle of his so that you never have to end; he's
deathproofed you—the grave has no power to stop
your life, and you are now free to live forever . . .
no question mark, no exclamation point, and abso-
lutely, no period

Where, O death, is your victory?
Where, O death, is your sting? (1 Corinthians 15:55)

Cemetery Visit   God gives life by taking away
death. To help your child understand how God is like
life itself, visit a cemetery. Walk quietly among the
graves; visit the gravesite of a loved one if you wish.
After a while, sit down on a bench and give your child
an opportunity to tell you what he's thinking. Ask,
"Is this scary for you? Is it sad? Why?" Get both

your and your child's feelings out in the open so you'll feel more comfortable about the setting.

Then turn the conversation toward death in general: "Why do people have to die? What happens to them when they do? Do they cease to exist, or do their minds continue on somehow?" To know whether or not there's life after death, it seems we'd have to talk to someone who's been there and come back. Can you think of anyone who's managed to do that? Why did Jesus go through all that pain and trouble?

Now talk about God's promise of a deathproof life. "Why does God want us to live forever? How can we be sure that He'll do what He says? Is there anything we need to do to hold up our end of the promise?"

Self-Portraits

> *O LORD, you brought me up from the grave;*
> *you spared me from going down into the*
> *pit.*   (Psalm 30:3)

> *I tell you the truth, whoever hears my word*
> *and believes him who sent me has eternal life*
> *and will not be condemned; he has crossed*
> *over from death to life.*   (Jesus, John 5:24)

30 ◆ God Is Like a Lifeguard

Practice Lifesaving

He reached down from on high and took hold of me; he drew me out of deep waters. (2 Samuel 22:17)

My friend Lanny prints and sells T-shirts. He makes a tanktop with the word LIFEGUARD printed across the front. It looks like the typical lifeguard shirt, until you read what is printed in smaller letters just above it: GOD IS MY.

It's not only a fun shirt—it's an accurate picture of God. To understand how God acts as our lifeguard, you need to understand what lifeguards are supposed to do.

Lifeguards have two duties. The first is to *guard* us from danger; the second is to *save* us if we get into trouble. The first duty compels them to post huge signs that say NO HORSEPLAY and to scream, "No running!" Without this duty to guard you from trouble, they could scream things like, "Go ahead and run —I have a first aid kit."

The second duty, to *save* us if we get into trouble, is just as important. It is their job to rescue us—even when we've ignored their advice and played with horses or slipped while running.

Lifeguard God performs these same two duties all the time. He guards us from all sorts of hazards, and He saves us when we get into trouble.

Hit the Water Take your child and one of his friends to the pool or beach. Tell them to pretend that they've just been hired as lifeguards: their first responsibility is to identify any hazards, and then to make up a list of rules to try to stop people from being hurt by them.

Unless you've discovered a secret swimming hole, a list of rules is probably posted nearby. With the kids, read the list and figure out the logic behind each of the rules. Any unnecessary rules? Any that should be added?

Next, get in the water and, if you know how, show the children some lifesaving skills. If you don't know the basics well enough to teach them, perhaps a lifeguard could help. When everyone is ready to rest a while, talk about Lifeguard God.

Here are some discussion ideas: "As head lifeguard for the planet, has God identified any hazards we should look out for? Has He posted a list of them anywhere? What's on that list? Has He made up any rules that are unnecessary?"

Ask, "If you do something you know is dangerous (shoplifting, skateboarding in busy parking lots), will

God still help you? How? If you obey all the rules, are you safe? Can you think of examples where God reaches out to save people from situations they didn't cause?"

Continue, "Can you think of an example in your own life where Lifeguard God guarded you from trouble or saved you from a bad situation? If He were sitting in a lifeguard tower right here, and He was about to warn you about some hazard in your life now, what would He say to you?

Other Perspectives *Give a Whistle.* If you've tried the above activity, you can give your child a whistle on a lanyard to remind him of the picture of God as his lifeguard.

Like a Bodyguard. A bodyguard is like a terrestrial lifeguard. His duties are to protect and to rescue the person he's guarding. Ask your child: "How is God like a personal bodyguard?"

Assistant Lifeguard. God can use each of us to help guard the lives of those around us. Ask your child to explain how he would be a lifeguard to a friend in each of these situations: a bad home life, a problem with drugs, in trouble with the law, being picked on at school.

31 ◆ God Is Like a Light

Turn Out the Lights

I am the light of the world. Whoever follows me will never walk in darkness, but will have the light of life.
(Jesus, John 8:12)

People aren't afraid of the dark—it's what's hidden in it that they worry about.

What hides in the dark? Lots of things: snakes, spiders, lizards, roaches, scorpions, bats, lions and tigers and bears (oh my), robbers, murderers, terrorists, monsters, aliens, ghosts, Bigfoot, Godzilla, King Kong, and the bogeyman.

That is just what's *outside* the body. Darkness on the inside is even scarier: evil thoughts, worries, fears; those nagging questions about death, value, purpose, love, failure. Life can seem like a room with no lights where you wander around blindly bumping into things. If you're lucky, you bump into good things. If you're unlucky, you bump into trouble.

The good news is that God has entered the room and switched on a light. He lights up our paths so we won't stumble. He shines into our brains (for me it's like a fog lamp) to help us make good decisions, to think clearly, to avoid heading into trouble. When we run into trouble anyway, He shines into our hearts, giving us the reason to go on.

Sit in the Dark   Here is a nighttime activity that will help your child understand how God is like a light. Tell your child that the two of you are going to do an experiment with light. Then remove the shade from a table lamp, set the lamp on the floor in the middle of the room, and turn it on. Draw the blinds, and turn off all the lights in the house. Sit next to each other beside the lamp (you may wish to reassure him that you're not going to scare him).

Tell your child you are going to switch the light off for a while but that you'll be there with him and will ask him some questions. Switch off the lamp. While sitting in the darkness, talk about light. Ask, "What does light do for us (lets us see, makes colors, illuminates dangers, takes away our fears of the unknown)? What don't you like about the dark? How does it make you feel?"

Now switch on the lamp. Ask, "How do you feel now? Why do you feel better when the light is on? How is God like a light? How does God take away fear? Does God turn His light on and off, or is it on all the time?"

Other Perspectives *Junior Lights.* In Matthew 5:14–16, Jesus claims that we are lights too. Read the verses together and figure out what we are supposed to do about it.

Self-Portraits

> *He is like the light of morning at sunrise*
>   *on a cloudless morning,*
> *like the brightness after rain*
>   *that brings the grass from the earth.*
> (2 Samuel 23:4)

> *The LORD is my light and my salvation—*
>   *whom shall I fear?* (Psalm 27:1)

> *Your word is a lamp to my feet*
>   *and a light for my path.*
> (Psalm 119:105)

> *In him was life, and that life was the light of men.* (John 1:4)

> *I have come into the world as a light, so that no one who believes in me should stay in darkness.* (Jesus, John 12:46)

32 ◆ God Is Like a Lion
Read a Lion's Tale

Do not weep! See, the Lion of the tribe of Judah, the Root of David, has triumphed.   (Revelation 5:5)

The picture of Jesus as a lion is a popular one, but you have to get all the way to the back of the Bible to find the only reference to it. Nonetheless, it's a wonderful picture, conveying two seemingly opposite impressions at the same time: beauty and terror.

Read   The best illustration of Jesus as a lion is in C.S. Lewis's classic children's fantasy work, The Chronicles of Narnia. The seven-book series takes you to Narnia, a world of kings and castles, talking animals, and a Christlike Lion named Aslan, son of the Emperor-Beyond-the-Sea. Each book is a complete story in itself, so you don't have to read the whole series.

The best way to read The Chronicles is by starting with book one: *The Lion, the Witch and the Wardrobe.* The story is exciting and fast-moving, so it's lots of fun to read aloud. Read a chapter a night, or gather around the fireplace and read several in one sitting. The parallels between Aslan and Jesus are numerous, so you'll have no problem painting a picture of God as a lion.

33 ◆ God Is Like a Listener
Listen Quietly

Before they call I will answer; while they are still speaking I will hear. (Isaiah 65:24)

Have you ever been talking on the phone when, in the middle of telling your story, you realize you haven't heard an "uh huh" or "really?" in the last minute or so? You start to wonder if the listener is there. Maybe she's set the phone down to turn on the TV or to make tuna salad. Or maybe she's still there, but not *there:* opening the mail, filing a nail, or drawing a moustache on the realtor's notepad photo.

Have you ever been talking to God and wondered the same thing? Maybe He's tired of hearing about your problems and requests. Or He's bored. Maybe he has too many people talking to Him at once—He's kicking Himself for creating a round world because it means it's always bedtime prayer time *somewhere* on the globe. This is silly conjecture, of course, but it brings up an important question: *When you're pouring out your heart to God, is He really listening?*

If the Bible is true, the answer is yes. God knows the frustration of talking to someone who isn't listen-

ing—we do it to Him every day—so He promises
again and again to listen to us whenever we call. And
sometimes, if you stay quiet long enough, God the
Listener becomes God the Voice.

Quiet Listening   Introduce your child to the
picture of God the Listener by teaching her to listen
quietly. Take the phone off the hook, turn off TVs,
stereos, and other noise makers, and sit together quietly for a couple of minutes. Take note of the sounds
you hear—the whir of the refrigerator, the house set-
tling, your own breathing, a neighbor's door slam, a
distant shout, a plane overhead.

Afterward, talk about the things you heard. Were
there any noises you've never noticed before? Were
there any you didn't recognize? Did you feel silly
sitting still? Did you feel uncomfortable?

Talk about God the Listener: Ask, "Did God hear
all those sounds? Does He hear every noise in the
world? How can He hear two noises or voices at the
same time? How many people can He hear at once?
When we pray to Him, does He hear all our prayers,
or just the important ones? How can you tell if He's
listening? Does He answer back? How do you listen
to God?"

Other Perspectives   *Silent Times.* Other
settings are good for quiet moments: a park, forest,
beach, near a stream. Be quiet at different times of

the day: sunrise, sunset, in place of grace before a meal.

Eye Listening.   Hold a silent family meal. From the moment you sit at the table until the meal is over, no talking. To communicate, use gestures; to listen, watch.

Self-Portraits

> *What other nation is so great as to have their*
> *gods near them the way the LORD our God is*
> *near us whenever we pray to him?*
> (Deuteronomy 4:7)

> *You hear, O LORD, the desire of the afflicted;*
> *   you encourage them, and you listen to their*
> *cry.*   (Psalm 10:17)

> *The eyes of the LORD are on the righteous*
> *   and his ears are attentive to their cry.*
> (Psalm 34:15)

34 ◆ God Is Like a Messenger
Deliver a Message

Then suddenly the Lord you are seeking will come to his temple; the messenger of the covenant, whom you desire, will come. (Malachi 3:1)

Let's say you had an important message for someone who just happened to live on the other side of the planet. How would you communicate? You can't call, because she doesn't have a telephone. You could send a letter, but the mail delivery between here and there is too slow; it could take months, or even get lost in the mail. You could try a telegram, but that's impersonal, and there's no signature to prove that it was really you who sent it. If the message is *really* important, there's only one way to send it: deliver it yourself.

God did that when He sent Jesus the Messenger to us. The message Jesus delivered was this:

My Dear Child,
*   I love you. I want you to live with Me forever. Hope to hear from you soon!*

*   All My love,*
*   God*

I'm paraphrasing, of course. The actual message was much longer, and Jesus said many other wonderful (and disturbing) things. The point is that the message was important enough for God to deliver Himself. He knew that "Long distance is the next best thing . . . ," but He couldn't settle for *next* best. It had to be the best, and that meant face to face.

Deliver   Let your child catch the picture of Messenger Jesus by being a messenger herself. Have her prepare a surprise message she can deliver to a parent or other family member while that person is at work. For example, help her bake cookies and rehearse a birthday message for her dad. Make sure he'll be at work when you arrive. Tell her to deliver the message in person. She might say something like, "I wanted to wish you a happy birthday in person. The message was too important to say over the phone."

On the way home, ask her how it went: "Was Dad surprised? How do you think he liked the message? Do you think he will remember this?" Then talk about Messenger Jesus: "Why did Jesus come to Earth? Couldn't God have just shouted from the sky? Why is it more special to have God deliver the message in person? What was His message?"

35 ◆ God Is Like a Mom
Take a Mom Survey

*As a mother comforts her child, so will
I comfort you . . .* (Isaiah 66:13)

Moms wrote the book on comfort. As a kid, if I came
in wet and shivering from the rain, my mother would
immediately get me out of wet clothes and into a hot
bath. Then Mom put my fresh clothes in the dryer so
they'd be toasty hot when I put them on. And there
might even be a cup of hot chocolate waiting for me
in the kitchen. By the time my mother was through
with me, I wasn't sure I'd ever been miserable at all.

God the Mom is like that. She takes us in from the
cold, bathes us in warmth, wraps us in comfort. She
lets us forget for a moment how cold the world can
be.

Mom Survey Conduct a survey following the
directions for Idea 12, God is Like a Dad, only use
the Mom Survey.

Mom Survey

What are the 3
most important responsibilities of a mom?

1. _____

2. _____

3. _____

What's your favorite part of being a mom?

_____

_____

_____

What's your *least* favorite thing about being a mom?

_____

_____

_____

36 ◆ God Is Like a Party Host
Check Out the Church Party

*I have come that they may have life,
and have it to the full.*
(Jesus, John 10:10)

Once upon a time, God decided to throw a party. He sent out invitations to His special friends. He made all the preparations and spared no expense. When it came time for the party, none of those He invited showed up. Some had other plans, some were too busy with work and family obligations, some stayed home to watch wrestling on TV. With all this food, a band, and decorations about to go to waste, God said, "Fine! If those I invited don't want to come, I'm going to invite *everyone*—complete strangers, bums off the street, anyone who wants to come."

The party is life with God. The guest list is no longer exclusive. Anyone invited can come and join in the celebration.

Church Party One of the reasons we go to church is to celebrate life with God. Explain to your child that church is kind of like a party. Talk about your own church: What kind of party is it?

The Guest List.   Who is invited to your church? Can anyone show up? Or are there only certain kinds of people who are accepted? Jesus invites everyone to the party, no one is too "uncool" for Him.

The Celebration.   The fact that we can actually live forever is something to get excited about! Does your church ever celebrate that? You don't have to wear party hats, crack open a piñata, or play pin the tail on the donkey, but does going to church ever seem like a celebration? God the Host fills our lives with joy and laughter.

The Host.   Does it seem like the ministers and teachers at your church are excited about holding a celebration? Or are they just doing it because they have to? God the Host wants to please us. He threw this party of life for us.

37 ◆ God Is Like a Potter

Play with Clay

Yet, O LORD, you are our Father. We are the clay, you are the potter; we are all the work of your hand.
(Isaiah 64:8)

Have you ever watched a potter at work? It's hard to decide what's more beautiful: the vessel formed from a lump of clay, or the dance the potter's hands perform to create it. She makes it look easy, but throwing a pot is difficult and delicate work. To make a pot, everything has to be right: the consistency of the clay, the wetness of her hands, the speed of the wheel, the thickness of the pot. If something is wrong, the pot collapses in her hands.

Even if she forms a beautiful pot, an air bubble hidden in the clay can explode while being fired, destroying her work—and everything else in the kiln. If her work survives the wheel and the kiln, the finished work of art is so delicate it will shatter if dropped or hit.

God is like a potter. He works long and hard to shape us into intricate and delicate forms. He carefully molds us into vessels that are both beautiful and useful. When He's finished forming us, our lives are as fragile as a clay pot.

Clay Play   Get some clay from an art supply store. You should be able to find the kind that can harden without a kiln. Don't bother trying to use a potter's wheel for this activity—they're hard to work with and frustrating to learn on. Instead, form bowls or other small objects using your hands. While you and your child are working, talk about God the Potter.

Self-Portraits

> *You turn things upside down, as if the potter were thought to be like the clay! Shall what is formed say to him who formed it, "He did not make me"? Can the pot say of the potter, "He knows nothing"?*   (Isaiah 29:16)

> *Does not the potter have the right to make out of the same lump of clay some pottery for noble purposes and some for common use?*   (Romans 9:21)

38 ◆ God Is Like a Priest

Make a Confession

For we do not have a high priest who is unable to sympathize with our weaknesses, but we have one who has been tempted in every way, just as we are—yet was without sin. Let us then approach the throne of grace with confidence, so that we may receive mercy and find grace to help us in our time of need.   (Hebrews 4:15,16)

Priests are spiritual middlemen, standing between a squeaky-clean God and dirty-behind-the-ears humans. In the Old Testament, priests offered the sacrifices and performed the rituals on behalf of the rest of the people. Because God was a stickler for detail, these middlemen had to be trained carefully and kept pure for their sacred duties.

Then along came Jesus, the ideal middleman. He's fully human, so He's qualified to speak for the human party; and He's fully God, so He represents the heavenly realm. He's the perfect priest, literally.

Here's a play-by-play look at how this new arrangement works: When you sin, you go to Jesus the Priest and confess (i.e., you admit your selfishness, express sorrow for disobeying God, ask for forgiveness). As a fellow human, He identifies with your struggle and hurts *with* you. He turns to God the Father and says, "I know this person, and I know what she's done. I've made the payment for her sin, and I wish to forgive her." God says, "Do it," then Jesus says to you: "Your sin is covered, you are forgiven." You're clean.

In religious talk, Jesus the Priest is our confessor, intercessor, atoner and forgiver, all wrapped in one. When you have business with God, Jesus is the one to talk to.

Confess   Here's an activity that can help your child understand the role of Jesus the Priest. To prepare, you'll need some flash paper, which is paper that burns completely when ignited, leaving no ashes or scraps. You can buy this wherever magic tricks are sold.

Both you and your child will need a sheet of flash paper. Explain that you both are to write notes of confession to Jesus: list your sins and ask Jesus to forgive you. After writing the notes fold them in half and put them in a bowl. Explain why you've written the notes to Jesus: because He's human and understands how we're tempted and can relate to our struggles. Explain that when we confess our sins to Him, He then goes to God the Father *for* us. God agrees that the sin was already paid for with Christ's sacrifice. Jesus then erases the sin and tells us we're forgiven.

Now light a match and toss it into the bowl. The paper, along with the sins, will vanish in a bright flash. Take a moment to thank God for His forgiveness. Talk about the experience: "Do you feel forgiven? How do you know if you really are? Do you think God photocopied our notes before they were destroyed? Why does God forgive us? Why do we talk to God through Jesus?"

Other Perspectives *Clean Slate.* If you
can't find flash paper, you can use regular paper and burn it in the fireplace or sink, or use a dry-erase board (wipe it, don't burn it), or use a word processor and just delete the document without saving it.

Self-Portraits

> *If we confess our sins, he is faithful and just and will forgive us our sins and purify us from all unrighteousness.*   (1 John 1:9)

39 ◆ God Is Like Rain

Go Puddle-Jumping

He will be like rain falling on a mown field, like showers watering the earth. (Psalm 72:6)

Rain is nature's way of taking a bath. It cleans the air, washes dust from the leaves, rinses off rocks and grass, flushes out streams. Rain makes the air smell better—or maybe it just washes away the things that make air smell bad. Rain makes seeds sprout, flowers bloom, and brown hillsides turn green.

God is like rain. He washes off the dirt and grime in our lives, He makes breathing fun. He refreshes us and brings new joy to our tired lives. He does it just by letting His grace fall on us.

Jump Puddles Take your kid puddle-jumping.* Put on raincoats (or cut head and arm holes in a couple of plastic trash bags) and head outside. Try to catch raindrops in your mouth. What do they taste like? Race sticks in the gutter. Try to stomp all the

---

* Contrary to what our moms told us, you don't catch a cold or flu by getting wet. You get into trouble when you stay wet too long and your body gets exhausted trying to keep warm: this lowers your body's defenses.

water out of a puddle. Stand on a street corner and wait for cars to drive through and drench you. Take a shower beneath a rain gutter.

Go to a playground. Glide down a wet slide. Try out the swings. Put your feet down and waterski across the puddle beneath the swing. Run and slide through a puddle in the grass. Hold a contest to see who can slide farther.

When you've had enough puddle jumping, head home and change into dry clothes. If the weather suits, light a fire in the fireplace and serve hot apple cider or hot chocolate. Talk about your adventure and how God is like rain.

Self-Portraits

> *Let my teaching fall like rain*
> * and my words descend like dew,*
> *like showers on new grass,*
> * like abundant rain on tender*
> *plants.*   (Deuteronomy 32:2)

> *Let us acknowledge the LORD;*
> * let us press on to acknowledge him.*
> *As surely as the sun rises*
> * he will appear,*
> *he will come to us like the winter rains,*
> * like the spring rains that water the*
> *earth.*   (Hosea 6:3)

40 ◆ God Is Like a Rescue Worker

Rehearse a Rescue

For he has rescued us from the dominion of darkness and brought us into the kingdom of the Son he loves. (Colossians 1:13)

A paramedic studies, trains, and rehearses long and hard for one job: to save lives. He saves babies, old people, friends, total strangers, handsome people, ugly people, heros, and criminals. It's his job.

That's Jesus's job too. He doesn't save just the rich or the good-looking or those with perfect church-attendance records. He saves anyone who calls out for Him.

Rescue Rehearsal To help your child see God as a rescue worker, give him the chance to be one himself. If he's old enough, take a first-aid course with him through your local Red Cross. Together you can practise the Heimlich maneuver to save someone from choking and how to perform rescue breathing. You will learn how to stop the bleeding from a major cut, what not to do with a back or neck injury, and what to do if someone swallows poison.

Conduct a family fire drill. Perhaps an older child can figure out how to help a younger sibling in case of fire. Demonstrate what the smoke alarm sounds like, show where the fire extinguisher is and how to use it, how to feel a door for heat before opening it, and how to stay low to minimize breathing smoke.

Talk about why it is important to know these things. Ask, "If you had the chance to rescue someone, would you do it? Why? Would you risk your own life to save someone else's? Why do some people such as firefighters and paramedics choose to make a living out of rescuing people?"

Now ask your child to compare God to a rescue worker. Ask, "How does God save people? What danger does He save them from? Why does He do it? Does He ever risk His own life to save someone? When someone is rescued by God, how does He feel?"

Other Perspectives *Ask a Rescuer Why.*
Call a fire station or ambulance company and ask if you and your child can stop by for a few minutes to interview a paramedic. Go to the station and talk to the paramedic about his work. Ask why he chose this profession; what he enjoys most; what's the worst part.

41 ◆ God Is Like a Rock

Go Climbing

From the ends of the earth I call to you, I call as my heart grows faint; lead me to the rock that is higher than I.
(Psalm 61:2)

A tsunami is a giant sea wave formed by an earthquake or volcanic eruption. In places like Hawaii, where tsunami warnings aren't uncommon, there's only one safe place to go—up. When the warning goes out, friends and neighbors meet on the hills and clifftops surrounding the town. If the tsunami hits the shore, it can wipe out anything at or near sea level—trees, houses, an entire town.

Life has its share of tsunamis, floods, tidal waves, and hurricanes. When these or other physical or emotional disasters strike, it's reassuring to know that our God is a solid and unmovable rock.

Climb a Rock Find some rocks you can climb with your child without either of you getting into danger. Scramble around for a while, trying different routes, exploring the cracks and crevices. When you get to the top, sit down together for a snack. Read the parable about the man who builds his house in the sand and the one who builds his on the rock (Luke 6:46–49). Talk about the meaning of the parable. Ask: "How is God like a rock?"

Self-Portraits

> *The LORD lives! Praise be to my Rock!*
> *Exalted be God, the Rock, my*
> *Savior!* (2 Samuel 22:47)

> *He lifted me out of the slimy pit,*
> *out of the mud and mire;*
> *he set my feet on a rock*
> *and gave me a firm place to*
> *stand.* (Psalm 40:2)

> *My salvation and my honor depend on God;*
> *he is my mighty rock, my*
> *refuge.* (Psalm 62:7)

> *Trust in the LORD forever,*
> *for the LORD, the LORD, is the Rock*
> *eternal.* (Isaiah 26:4)

42 ◆ God Is Like a Roommate
Tour the House

I pray that out of his glorious riches he may strengthen you with power through his Spirit in your inner being, so that Christ may dwell in your hearts through faith.   (Ephesians 3:16, 17)

When you invite Christ to be a part of your life, He comes to live in your "heart." A brilliant illustration of this idea was written by Robert Munger in a booklet called *My Heart, Christ's Home* (1954, Inter-Varsity Press), a story of a man who invited Christ to live in his heart.

When Christ moves into the man's heart, the two take a tour: they check out the library (his mind), dining room (appetites and desires), workshop (work), as well as other important rooms in his life. The man soon discovers that his new roommate has His own ideas about how these rooms ought to be used. With the man's permission, Christ transforms the man's heart, room by room, into a warm and beautiful home.

House Tour   Get a copy of *My Heart, Christ's Home* to read to your child. As you read each section of the story, walk into the room of your house that corresponds with that section. You may have to improvise—a desk can act as the study, for example. As you tour the house, feel free to set the story aside to talk about the messages as they apply to your child's life. Ask her about the rooms in her own heart. What would Jesus say as He walked into *her* dining room, *her* library?

43 ♦ God Is Like a Servant

Be a Butler

Who, being in very nature God, did not consider equality with God something to be grasped, but made himself nothing, taking the very nature of a servant. (Philippians 2:6, 7)

Throughout time, governments and companies around the world have developed organizational charts with the head honcho (queen, president, dictator, grand poobah) at the top, with lesser honchos arranged at various levels beneath.

Along comes Jesus, who flips the whole thing upside down: the first will be last, the exalted will be humbled, and all sorts of other convoluted ideas about leadership. True to style, Jesus didn't stand in a pulpit and preach the virtues of servanthood. Instead, He got down on His hands and knees and washed people's feet.

Be a Butler Together with your child, serve a formal meal to the rest of the family. Dress up as formal waiters, with dress pants, white shirts, and ties. Prepare the dinner table with a tablecloth, candles, and your best dishes. Fold the napkins into strange shapes like they do at fancy restaurants. Oh yes—don't forget to make a nice meal.

Seat family members when they arrive for dinner; place napkins on their laps, pour water, serve the food, and generally hover over them during the meal. After the main course, clear the dishes and serve dessert. If you've done well, maybe you'll get a big tip.

Afterward, talk with your child about how it felt to be a servant. Then talk about God the Servant: what He's done to serve us and how He demonstrated servanthood.

Other Perspectives *Foot Bath.* It's hard to imagine Jesus getting down on His hands and knees to wash twenty-four feet in the middle of dinner! But that's what He did to teach servanthood, and you may want to try the gesture to convey the same message. The washing instructions appear in John 13:1–13.

Self-Portraits

> *"If anyone wants to be first, he must be the very last, and the servant of all."*
> (Jesus, Mark 9:35)

44 ◆ God Is Like a Shepherd
Take Care of a Pet

I am the good shepherd. The good shepherd lays down his life for the sheep. (Jesus, John 10:11)

I have no problem imagining God as a shepherd. The part I have trouble with is admitting that I'm a sheep. It's not a flattering metaphor. Sheep seem preoccupied with one thing: feeding themselves. They seem stupid, easily frightened, and prone to wandering into trouble. Okay, so the metaphor is accurate. At least there's some comfort in knowing that, if I have to play the part of a sheep, Jesus is willing to play the part of the shepherd.

Pet Care You may not have a paddock of sheep at your house, but if you have a pet, you can use it to help create the picture of God the Shepherd. Help your child fill out the chart, "Responsibilities of a Good Pet Owner."

When he's done with this chart, help him fill in the second chart, "Responsibilities of God the Shepherd."

Responsibilities of a
Good Pet Owner

Pet's name: _____ Age: _____

Type of animal: ☐ dog ☐ cat ☐ fish

☐ other _____ ☐ rabbit ☐ snake ☐ zebra

NEED	RESPON-SIBILITY	WHEN & HOW OFTEN	WHAT HAPPENS IF YOU FORGET
FOOD			
SHELTER			
HEALTH			
LOVE & ATTENTION			

Responsibilities of
God the Shepherd

Sheep's name (that's you!): _____ Age: ____

Type of sheep: ☐ewe ☐ram

NEED	RESPON-SIBILITY	WHEN & HOW OFTEN	WHAT HAPPENS IF GOD FORGETS
FOOD			
SHELTER			
HEALTH			
LOVE & ATTENTION			

45 ◆ God Is Like a Shield

Stage a Newspaper Battle

The LORD is my strength and my shield; my heart trusts in him, and I am helped. (Psalm 28:7)

A shield is like a portable fortress that you can hide behind for protection in battle. Because it's portable, you can use it when you're on the offense; a fortress is strictly for defense. A shield gives a warrior more confidence because he can attack with less fear of being hurt. It doesn't make the battle a cinch—a stray arrow can hit you from the side, and a crushing blow from a sword or ax can break the arm holding the shield. Still, it makes a battle a little less dangerous.

God is like a shield. He goes with us in life, helping to protect us from attack.

Paper Battle To demonstrate the power of a shield, stage a newspaper battle in the house. You and your child each build a shield out of thick cardboard. You can make handles by poking a few holes in the right places and looping small pieces of rope through the back. Decorate the shields with paint or colored pens. If you don't care to make your own shields, you can use trash can lids.

Once you have your shields, you'll need to make your weapons. Each side gets a stack of newspapers. Make paper grenades by wadding up sheets of newspaper. Now mark off some kind of line down the middle of the room, stand on your respective sides, and start firing by throwing the soft paper wads at each other.

Play two rounds of two minutes each. Fight the first round without your shields, the second one with them. To keep score, count the number of times you manage to hit your opponent's body, or just see who has the least amount of paper on her side of the room at the end of the round.

When you've had enough, call a truce, clean up the papers, and then go wash the newspaper ink off your hands. Talk about the shields. Were they helpful? How many times were you hit without your shield? With it? Now talk about God: How is He like a shield?

Self-Portraits

> *My shield is God Most High,*
> *who saves the upright in heart.*
> (Psalm 7:10)

46 ◆ God Is Like a Sword

Study Swords

When I sharpen my flashing sword and my hand grasps it in judgment, I will take vengeance on my adversaries and repay those who hate me.
(Deuteronomy 32:41)

Let's face it: our God is deadly. It's not the kind of thing we like to talk about; it's much nicer to think of God as a kind and forgiving daddy. But He's a big God, with many sides to His character. At times He reveals the side that wields a sword.

The good news is that, because God is like an avenging sword, we don't have to be. We humans aren't strong enough to avenge our enemies without becoming like them ourselves. God wields the sword of vengeance because He knows that we can't pick it up without cutting ourselves.

Sword Study   Until this century, swords were standard issue for all soldiers. You still see them worn by soldiers in parade uniform. Check out a book on swords from the library, or visit the weapons display at a museum. Discuss with your child the different kinds of swords—straight bladed, foils, double-edged, lancets, sabers, scimitars—who used them, and how they fought with them. Then talk about God the Sword.

Self-Portraits

It is mine to avenge; I will repay.
 In due time their foot will slip;
their day of disaster is near
 and their doom rushes upon them.
(Deuteronomy 32:35)

Take the helmet of salvation and the sword of the Spirit, which is the word of God.
(Ephesians 6:17)

For the word of God is living and active. Sharper than any double-edged sword, it penetrates even to dividing soul and spirit, joints and marrow; it judges the thoughts and attitudes of the heart.
(Hebrews 4:12)

For we know him who said, "It is mine to avenge; I will repay," and again, "The Lord will judge his people." It is a dreadful thing to fall into the hands of the living God.
(Hebrews 10:30, 31)

47 ◆ God Is Like a Teacher

Play Teacher

In a culture where the religious instructors prided themselves in delivering obtuse lectures, pointless arguments, and long-winded prayers, Jesus was a renegade teacher. He avoided long messages; instead He told colorful stories, asked plenty of questions, left people begging for more (when's the last time you wished the sermon was longer?). He was a master of multimedia, using sight, sound, taste, touch and smell to make a message unforgettable (feeding the five thousand, the Last Supper). Most important, He loved his students, and they knew it.

Professor Jesus was a master teacher. We have much to learn from what He taught *and* how He taught it.

Play Teacher Set up a classroom at home with you as the student and your child as the teacher. Ask her to prepare a short lesson for you on a subject she knows well, such as how to use a dictionary, how to divide, state geography, the meaning of a certain Bible passage, anything she feels confident to teach.

While she's the teacher, stay in character as a student. You can ask lots of questions, but don't tell her how to teach and don't use this time to correct her if she makes a mistake (but if she tries to send you to the principal's office, send her to her room).

At the end of the lesson, ask her what it was like to be a teacher. Ask, "How did you feel? Was it fun? Frustrating?" Ask her to identify what makes a good teacher or a bad teacher. Then talk about Professor Jesus. Ask, "What kind of teacher was Jesus? How do you know? What teaching methods did Jesus use to get His message across? How did He treat His students?"

48 ◆ God Is Like a Team Captain
Choose Sides

But you are a chosen people, a royal priesthood, a holy nation, a people belonging to God, that you may declare the praises of him who called you out of darkness into his wonderful light.
(1 Peter 2:9)

Many of us have had this experience at one time in our lives: They're choosing teams for a game of some sort, and the two team captains are standing in front of a crowd of prospective team members. The captains alternate picking people from the crowd. They each pick their best friends on the first round, and their next best friends on round two. Then they search the crowd for the best players, each captain being accosted by a dozen waving hands and the pleas of "Pick me!"

As the crowd thins out, the kids who've been picked are obviously the lucky ones. Cries of "Pick me!" sound desperate now.

There are just a few kids left. No one bothers to beg, but on the inside you're all praying, "Don't let me be last—again." Now there are four left—a 25 percent chance. Now a one-in-three chance. Now it's fifty-fifty. Then it's just you—your pleas went unanswered.

Now the two team captains start arguing. It seems there's an uneven number of players—you're the odd one—and neither wants to get stuck with you. The loser of the argument grimaces and calls you over. Oh joy.

The Bible says that God chooses you to be on His team. So if you've ever experienced anything like the above, you may think God chooses you because He *has to:* "After all, I'm God. I'm *supposed* to pick him. It's in My contract." Or maybe you think He picks you because He's a nice God and He *feels sorry* for you: "If I don't pick him, who else will?" But it's not like that. Captain God chooses you because He *wants you.* He wants you on His team.

Last Pick   Ask your child to recall a time when he was chosen last, or nearly so. Ask him to describe what it felt like and why he was picked last. Ask him if he's ever been picked first, or nearly so, and what that felt like. Ask him why he was chosen first. Now explain that he has been picked for a team—God's team. Ask, "Why do you think God picked you? What can you do for Him, now that you are on His team?"

49 ◆ God Is Like a Tower

Get Tall

The name of the LORD is a strong tower; the righteous run to it and are safe. (Proverbs 18:10)

When I was about ten years old I managed to talk my big sister into taking me to the beach with her friends for a day. As soon as we got there, I waded out into the surf up to my waist. When I looked up, I saw a massive wave preparing to break in front of me. I panicked. I tried to scramble for the beach, but the undertow pulled my feet out from under me and started to drag me under the breaking wave. I called out for help.

My sister's friend was standing several yards away. Jim, who was nearly seven feet tall, ran to me, yanked me out of the water and over the top of the wave just as it broke. How small the wave looked from up there. It was the same wave; the only thing that had changed was my perspective.

God is like a tower: tall, magnificent, indestructible. His tower doesn't lean, and He doesn't even charge admission. The view from the top convinces

you that even your biggest problem is much smaller
than God.

Tall Trip   Visit a tower with your child. If you
live near a big city, there's probably an observation
deck in one of the tall buildings. Or just look for
anything with a view: an office building, apartment
tower, or mountain overlook. Talk about the feelings
of being up high. Ask, "Does being up high make you
feel stronger or more powerful? Is it scary? Why do
people build tall buildings? How is God like a tower?"

Self-Portraits

> *From the ends of the earth I call to you,*
> *I call as my heart grows faint;*
> *lead me to the rock that is higher than I.*
> *For you have been my refuge,*
> *a strong tower against the foe.*
> (Psalm 61:2, 3)

50 ◆ God Is Like a Vine

Find a Vine

I am the vine; you are the branches. If a man remains in me and I in him, he will bear much fruit; apart from me you can do nothing.
(Jesus, John 15:5)

Grapes don't actually grow from grape vines, they grow from branches attached to the vine. The vine itself may be over a hundred years old, but the branches are new with each season.

God is like a grape vine. He doesn't grow fruit directly; He grows and nurtures good branches to bear the fruit for Him. You're one of His branches. Stay attached to Him, and He'll send you what you need to grow good fruit. Break off from God and the fruit dies, you die, and God ends up with less fruit. It's a bad deal all around. Stay connected.

Vine Find You can help your child see this botanical picture of God by showing him a real vine in action. If you can't locate a grape vine, look for some kind of berry vine. If vines are hard to find where you live, a fruit tree will do. Explain how the vine grows branches for bearing fruit. Point out how the vine nurtures the branches so they can grow strong enough to hold the weight of the fruit yet be flexible enough to survive shaking in the wind.

Look for a branch that's broken off the vine. Have your child estimate the chances that this branch will bear fruit. Now talk about God the Vine: "If God is the vine, who are the branches? What are the fruit? How do we keep growing good fruit?"

Other Perspectives   *Fruit-of-the-Vine Picnic.*
Put together a picnic lunch made from grapes: peanut butter sandwiches with grape jelly, grapes, raisins, grape juice, raisin bread. Talk about how grapes grow and how God is like a vine.

51 ◆ God Is Like a Voice

Name that Voice

The voice of the LORD is powerful; the voice of the LORD is majestic.
(Psalm 29:4)

The portable audiotape recorder was invented about nineteen hundred years too late to catch God's voice on tape. If we'd gotten His voice on tape that day by the Jordan River when He said, "This is My Son . . . ," we'd know whether His voice is really as deep and echoey as it sounds in all those old movies. (A recording would almost certainly prove that He never spoke with a slight British accent, and that he never even spoke in English.)

Except for occasional tabloid reports ("God Spoke Through My Toaster—in Dutch!") we don't hear about God speaking out loud to people anymore. It was a rare thing even in biblical times. God saves His audible declarations for special occasions—birth of His nation, dictating the ten commandments, His son's baptism, stuff like that.

He prefers to speak to people in less spectacular ways, using prophets, teachers, friends, family, circumstances, and times of inner silence and prayer to speak to our hearts.

Guess Who's Talking   To help your child think about what it means to recognize God's voice, show her how well she knows other people's voices. Using a portable tape recorder, make two-second recordings of ten people you think your child might know. You can tape the voices of characters from TV shows and movies, the President in a news conference, a popular singer, sports announcers, an aunt's or a friend's voice over the phone. When you've gotten all ten recordings, you are ready to play the game with her.

Tell her the object is to see how many of the ten voice samples she can correctly identify (you'll be amazed). Talk about how remarkable it is that in two seconds she can identify the owner of the voice from among the hundreds of voices she knows. Ask how she thinks that's possible?

Now talk about God's voice. Ask, "Have you ever heard God's voice? How do you know? How does God speak to you? What kinds of things does He say?"

52 ◆ God Is Like Water

Start a Water Fight

O God, you are my God, earnestly I seek you; my soul thirsts for you, my body longs for you, in a dry and weary land where there is no water.
(Psalm 63:1)

In hot dry weather you need to drink two gallons of water per day just to keep going. It's no wonder. Your body uses water for everything—temperature control, digestion, air filtering, waste disposal, cell manufacture, and if you're under age two, drooling. In fact, your body is about 70 percent water.

God is like water. He cools and refreshes, quenches our desires, flushes out all the junk in our lives. That is, He does all this if we take and drink Him.

Wet Fun Water fights are easy to start on a hot day. For example, you and your child could wash the car together. While your child is hosing off the car, "accidentally" walk into the spray. With mock seriousness, accuse him of trying to get you wet, then start to walk toward him with that give-me-the-hose look. If he's like most kids, he'll give it to you—in the face. Run for a bucket you've stashed behind the car, then charge him with it. If he drops the hose, pick it up and start spraying him. The rest of the battle is up to the two of you.

When you're through soaking each other, dry off and recount the game play-by-play. Talk about why water is so much fun. Talk about why it's so important to us physically. Then talk about the idea that God is like water. Ask, "In what way is God like water? What happens when you 'pour' God into your life? What does that mean? How do you keep from becoming dehydrated?"

Self-Portraits

As the deer pants for streams of water,
so my soul pants for you, O God. My soul
thirsts for God, for the living God.
When can I go and meet with God?
(Psalm 42:1, 2)
Everyone who drinks this water will be thirsty
again, but whoever drinks the water I give
him will never thirst. Indeed, the water I give
him will become in him a spring of water
welling up to eternal life.
(Jesus, John 4:13, 14)